FORTY YEARS OF INDIAN POLICE

FORTY YEARS OF INDIAN POLICE

TRILOK NATH

CONCEPT PUBLISHING COMPANY
NEW DELHI

First Published 1981

Trilok Nath (*b*. 1916-)

Published by

Naurang Rai
Concept Publishing Company
H-13, Bali Nagar
NEW DELHI-110015 (India)

Printed by

Kay Pee Composing Agency
at Kiran Mudran Kendra, Mayapuri
New Delhi-110064.

INTRODUCTORY

TOWARDS the end of my thirtysix years of service in the Indian Police, I was appointed Chairman of a Committee to formulate a blue-print for a reorganized Police in Bihar State. I was also to prepare in this context a new police manual. This exercise was long overdue, as the extant manual was framed sixty years ago. Against this backdrop, I was requested by my friends to write my memoirs of the Police after my retirement. These friends were aware that I had expressed in the Press some unconventional views on police reorganisation soon after independence came, which had earned me official displeasure as the views were too radical. I had later written a series of articles for the Press pseudonymously, which attracted considerable attention and which were well received by the people. However, rather than embark on this work on my retirement, I put in a series of articles on various facets of the police and with these as base, produced a book on the working of the police, the history of police functions, and what according to me should be the shape of things to come. This book received the approbation of Lok Nayak Jai Prakash Narayan, who volunteered to write its Foreword. Thereafter, I found it possible to write up some thirty stories of interesting crimes from all parts of India indicating the procedures of their investigation. Having got over this, I felt that I could now try my hand at recording some vignettes of my experience in the Police which would include departmental matters, the uncovering of the perpetrators of sensational crimes, the part played by the Police in the social milieu after the attainment of independence, and also the political happenings with which the police service in the country was kneaded, being the prime intelligence and peace keeping organisation of the State. This force provided the cement of the social fabric. All this could provide ample material of interest.

The result is this book. I have started with my experience as a youngster struggling through the educational processes to find a place in the police apex service. I have delineated interesting experiences of later dates which indicate the built-up of the Police and its auxiliaries, the social and political pulls, the ideological confusion which independence brought in the minds of the intelligentsia, and the hesitancy peculiar to an educated Indian. I have given only as much of the biographical details as was necessary for the proper delineation of the incidents.

I feel sure that these pages will be of interest both to the professional policemen and to the lay-reader. In this country, the Police is no longer merely a general administrative cadre, which it was when I joined the department. This service is now assuming, though rather slowly, the position of a specialist. When this happens fully its working would be anathema to those not in it. Therefore, so far my period of the service is concerned, there should be a general interest in matters with which I dealt. I have not touched on my experiences in the post-retirement period. Emergency was declared in the country a few months after my retirement and this unprecedented event produced many an interesting situation. Later a National Police Commission came into being, followed by a mutiny of the police forces. All this will deserve separate notice.

I wish specially to place on record my thanks to the publisher for taking on this work at short notice. There have been numerous difficulties but they have tackled them effectively and have indeed done a fine job.

CONTENTS

1

EARLY EXPERIENCES

MY FIRST brush with the gigantic administrative machine in the country, which at that time meant the Police, was towards the close of the third decade of this century when I was barely twelve years of age. Public feeling had been considerably ruffled, bordering on exasperation, at the failure of the ruling powers even to meet half way the demands of the people for the recognition of their very existence. The Simon Commission was set up in 1928 as a sop to the aspirations of the people. Its members made a visit to the country to assess the strength of public opinion over the demand for self-government. Demonstrations broke out all over the country and some of these sparked off violent action from the minions of the law ; these hardly fitted in with the protestations of the government and their desire to help in fulfilling the people's aspirations. These demonstrations were arranged at almost all the points which the Commission touched, and were a matter of prestige for the political parties and in particular the Congress which had spearheaded all anti-government agitations. The attempt on the part of the local authorities, however, was to show to the Commission as if no opposition existed. The hour of arrival of the Commission, was kept a closely guarded secret so that a large conglomeration of people could not possibly be organized. Yet the organisers of the protests lay in wait hours before the likely hour of their arrival. At Patna, capital city of the province of Bihar and Orissa —Orissa had not yet been carved out—this visit was to take place on a cold wintry morning. Realising that the special train schedule may be changed, the entire demonstrating crowd rallied near the ceremonial platform of the Patna railway station from the previous evening. The presence of large bodies of policemen in the neighbourhood of the railway station from the evening itself gave a clear indication that something was in the offing. Perhaps the Indian counterpart of the Commission would arrive. The crowd was kept away at a respectable distance from the railway platform within the Hardinge Park, which had been set up in memory of Lord Hardinge, India's Viceroy, who faced the bomb of an anarchist at Delhi. The attempt of the demonstrators was to approach as near the ceremonial platform as possible, in the hope that the slogan shouting would arouse the members of the Commission from their sleep, in the comfortable railway saloons. There was the usual ding-dong movement, the crowd surging forward and often driven back by police lathis. The result : severe injuries to some of the demonstrators including Rajendra Babu who was in the forefront. Some liberal leaders also came in their cars to mark their presence : people like Hassan Imam, one-time Executive Councillor and a judge of the High Court, and his wife Nellie Imam were also there. They too had a taste of it. The melee resulted in considerable bruises to youngsters like us also who had gone for fun and excitement rather than for any purposive participation in the demonstration. As the crowd was pushed back, some of us got entangled in thorny bushes and had a taste of the barbed wire as well which had been spread in some areas. The barbed wire was fixed provocatively and helped only to add fuel to the fire. The army known in the area was the British Unit located in the nearby cantonment at Danapur. To our young minds the police appeared to be a minor version of this army, but this police force was all Indian and included some up-country Pathans with whom I was not unfamiliar, as my father had come along from distant Punjab to his assignment in Bihar. And during our periodical visits to the Punjab we saw a lot of them. We found this motley civil army—the police, led by British Sergeants, who appeared to us as army officers. I was to learn later that these Sergeants were retired Subalterns of the British army who lorded it over the *sipahis* of the police. This system kept British subordinates in direct touch with the policemen and through them with the mass of the people. The nonchalance with which these *sahibs* dealt blows on the otherwise completely non-violent crowd, gave us a rude shock. Nevertheless the pressure of the crowd from behind was mainly responsible for thrusting those in the front against the barbs causing serious injuries to them. The governmental agencies therefore affirmed that they were not responsible for all this as the crowd should have realised the result of their own enthusiasm. Next morning the local press carried news of the demonstration. We got the story : the hour of arrival of the Commission had been so arranged that the vanguard of the Commission alone could have a taste of the demonstration and the "foreign" members, having arrived earlier, had left for the Government House. The Indian counterpart of the Commission arrived according to schedule and had seen and heard the demonstrators. The strong feelings of the people in general could not, however, have remained unknown to the members of the Commission. Rajendra Babu had comparatively minor injuries, but the violence later inflicted on the demonstrators at Lahore was to result in the death of Lala Lajpat Rai. This was reported as the last nail on the coffin of the British Imperial rule. The picture of the police to my young mind was therefore one of oppression and high-handedness. They appeared to be a lot of sadists. Another visual symbol was the unkempt traffic policeman, who was the invariable butt of ridicule and lampoons. We also understood that some police constables performed patrols at night and caught prowlers. But of this we had no experience and returning home late some nights from a dinner, we did see some ill-clad *khaki* uniformed men in the background of dim gas lights. But that was about all.

The Boy-Scout movement was fostered greatly under the wings of the administration and encouraged regimentation and training of young boys to make them suitable citizens who would take the oath of loyalty to the King of England and the government as established by law. Boy Scouts, and cubs were required to dress up in the army *khaki* and were drilled and instructed by *khaki* clad instructors drawn from the safe sectors of the population. I remember that the Boy Scout Commissioner of the province then was the Chaplain of the cantonment, a fully paid government functionary. As a cub I, along with the other members of our troop, were required to line the route to welcome the visiting Viceroy. It was arranged that the Viceroy would step out of the motorcade near the Government House at Patna, where we would be located, to greet us. This was intended to show to us the administration's solicitude for children. The headquarters pack of the cubs in fact consisted entirely of children of select government officials. When the rehearsals were arranged, I found this highly degrading as it appeared that we were to behave like the flunkeys of the *sahibs* and take on the role of the police constables lining the route. I declined to go to the final event and this nearly caused a catastrophe at home. My father appeared to be greatly embarrassed but nothing would move me. Later I gave up attending the parades and the cub meets. I understood that official displeasure was conveyed to my father for all this.

The visits by distinguished personages like the Viceroy or the provincial Governor, were occasions for displaying the police. There were also stories that a large number of persons belonging to the C.I.D. (Police) were deployed to keep watch over political agitators, a section of whom was avidly taking to violent means to attain their objectives, Mahatma Gandhi's teachings notwithstanding. In the early years of the third decade in 1931, I was on a visit to the hill resort of Solan, half-way between Kalka and Simla, the summer headquarters of the Imperial Government at Delhi. I was staying as a guest of Dr. Sachchidanand Sinha being the schoolmate of his son Radhakrishan. Dr. Sinha had inherited a fine house in this hill resort. With his vast experience and contacts—he was an ex-Executive Councillor of the Bihar provincial administration—the house was the centre of attraction for the concourse visiting Simla from the plains. It was by all standards a safe place. We were watching the Viceroy's motorcade pass by this residence. Quite by accident, a chunk of the rock wall from the hillside fell on the car route as the procession passed. This was sufficient provocation for a protracted investigation by plain clothesmen, who arrived at the residence of Dr. Sinha. Apparently nothing untoward could have happened in this safe locality but the enquiries were directed towards finding out if the young boys from distant Bihar could have attempted to throw a missile at the motorcade. At Patna, my father was mighty worried. We were a middleclass family, which had made a niche for itself in the administrative cadre and the younger members of the family were expected to find their places in due course, at senior government levels. My father was apprehensive lest this freak accident of nature in which a stone fell on the road, might turn out to be a permanent mark against us when it came to absorption in government employment. But we were informed that all this greatly depended on the trend of the C.I.D. report. The impression therefore in our minds about the police was that of a powerful group which could foist the responsibility of any event on any person that suited its whims. I was told later, when we returned to Patna, that the incident had assumed a serious complexion and it was the intercession of Dr. Sinha, which had eased matters. We had our contacts with the nationalist elements who frequently visited our house for help on various occasions. The editor of a local nationalist journal Murli Babu informed my father that he could obtain information about the plans of the administration from the police subordinates of the C.I.D. and these minions of the law also arranged to furnish some information to their bosses of the happenings in the other camp. It was clear that the subordinates of the Criminal Investigation Department were playing a double game, obtaining the confidence of the ruling powers and yet working hand in glove with the nationalist anti-government groups. To our minds, therefore, the added impression about the police was of a set of double dealers, who could not be relied on. We had a story in this connexion from the Punjab which was often repeated. It implied a serious castigation of the entire police force. This story stated that an Indian sepoy of the army returning home on annual leave was told by the tonga driver, as he drove home from the railway station, that the sepoy's wife had been blessed with a son. When reminded by the police constable, who was also travelling on the same tonga, that the sepoy was married only a few months back, he quipped with the reply that he was not worried as after all the new arrival would be enlisted as a police constable in due course.

Amongst the earlier memories, is a visit to Patna by Gandhiji, to attend a meeting of the All India Congress Committee. This meeting was held in a *maidan* not far from our house. There was a khadi exhibition, with which was allied a drive for collection of funds. It was advertised that the funds would be used for the welfare of Harijans and the downtrodden. This gathering had little uniformed police attention and yet we could sense that the place must be teeming with plainclothed C.I.D. agents, the type who had tried to put us in the wrong box at Solan. We were not surprised to see some policemen of the local police station in civilian attire. They were also contributing money when the call for funds was made. Such public exhibition of sympathy did evoke a favourable response in our mind, but this was greatly marred when a sudden search was effected in our neighbourhood in the house of one of our schoolmates. These boys worked actively with the volunteer corps rigged up by the Congress leaders on this occasion. The idea was to discourage young boys from participating in the working of the volunteer corps. But the search far from being a deterrent encouraged a larger group of boys to join the ranks of volunteers. An Inspector of Police, who come to our house sometimes, was heard to make a statement that the future of the boys who take part in the volunteer body was sealed and it would affect the career of the parents as well. This officer was a much respected member of the local Indian community. And the Indian content of the superior ranks in the police was so little that the Inspector really could be considered as the representative of the upper Indian society in the police. This officer would wax eloquent on the virtues of his British seniors recounting stories of how they helped their Indian subordinates, even sending monthly monetary subsidies to their families. This could apparently have added to the fund of loyalty for the Crown in the subordinate police ranks. The picture presented to us thus was of a benign oligarchy, who quite unlike the Indian landlords, who had no consideration for the welfare of the poor cultivators, took a benevolent interest in their subordinates. We were also aware of the discourteous and rough behaviour of the Indian policemen of subordinate ranks. In contrast the impression created of the British seniors was that of a benign lot, who kept their distance from their Indian subordinates, yet dispensed even-handed justice.

In 1934 the profile of the police came into prominence before me during one of the journeys to the Kulu Valley. The area was difficult of access : there was merely a single track roadway leading into the heart of this valley. A bus ride on this route had a very large element of hazard, though interesting as one had a gorgeous view of the virgin mountains and valleys overflowing with flowers and fruit. On this journey I was witness to a tiff between the bus driver and a local schoolmaster. The bus driver referred to the schoolmaster as a petty underling whose scale of emoluments classed him below the chaprasis. However, the consideration paid to the personal servant of a senior British official travelling by the same bus, was a sad contrast. This servant took up the case of the schoolmaster and threatened to place the driver on the mat before his master. He said he would so manoeuvre that the *sahib* would get annoyed with the bus operator and this would put the bus driver in trouble. A Sub-Inspector of police travelling by the same bus also recounted his own experience vis-a-vis the British elements in the police indicating that he was really performing the job of a sweeper. He enjoyed little respect in the eyes of the higher echelons of the administration. The story was in complete contrast to the Inspector's story, which I had heard at home. All this resulted in some confusion in my mind. There was clear indication of malfunctioning of the police force, which lacked cohesion and of which the morale was definitely low particularly in subordinate ranks which appeared to act as the strong arm of the administration.

About this time I was also confronted with the version of a senior teacher in the college, who belonged to the Indian Educational Service. Commenting on the type of duties the police was required to perform and the reputation that this force had earned for illegal earnings and atrocious behaviour, this senior luminary of the Education Department gave vent to his feelings stating that service in all ranks of the police in the country was a most degrading experience. It was a clear case of a sell-out of one's conscience and in the view of this senior educationist, the result was bound to be adverse. *Karma* of this variety would not earn emancipation. He said that his father, himself a senior civil servant, had said that a stint in the police service would mean the end of the family lineal tree, as the work done was accursed.

The Darbar Day was observed in a big way at Patna as was possibly done in all the provincial capitals in the country. This day synchronised with the holding of an investiture by King George V at Delhi, when the country's political capital was shifted from Calcutta. On this occasion select Indians mainly of the official fraternity, and a few of the landed aristocracy, which constituted the total of the upper stratum of society, were invited. They all had to sport the English type of attire, tail coats and all. Only a few conservative Zamindars would dress in *achkan* and turban. Hectic preparations for this function used to be made in our house well in advance so that my father could attend the function in full official regalia. But to us the interesting item was the police parade which was held in the local *maidan*, previously a race course. This *tamasha* could be enjoyed by all from the common stand, but there were blocks reserved for students and we could avail of these. Weeks before the parade, we were also spectators of the smartly turned out police subordinates which included up-country Pathans, some of them mounted, who moved regularly to the parade ground for rehearsals. Their turnout and discipline impressed us greatly. We would all have liked this discipline to get implanted in the schools and colleges. The physical training classes and compulsory games in our schools were an eye wash and the modicum of training given under the aegis of the university training corps, was not worth learning as it involved considerable waste of time with no commensurate benefits. The feeling had also grown that this training was merely an attempt at regimenting the life of the youth. Considering that the show of the Congress volunteers at their annual function, compared to the display in the police parades was extremely poor, we had a feeling that the indigenous training devices were inadequate. But with all the faults, the police service appeared to provide avenues for solving the problems confronting us and of helping the poor citizen.

Netaji Subhash Chandra Bose came on a visit to Patna. He was then the President of the A.I.C.C. He stayed with his brother, a barrister-at-law practising at the Patna High Court. Netaji's nephew Dwijen, later to become an important leader of the Forward Bloc, was my classfellow at school and I was tempted to go to his house in order to see Netaji at close quarters. The youthful Netaji had a host of Congress volunteers surrounding him and though being near the leader enthused us, the volunteers, some of whom were well-known rowdies in the student circles, disturbed me greatly. It was amusing to see a large number of police constables lounging round the residence and this house was located right across the road from the Kotwali police station. That Netaji gave up a cushy career in the Indian Civil Service to plunge into the freedom movement, was attractive and lent him the aura of a matinee idol but the men surrounding him provided a damper to this image. It did fortify my belief that it would require herculean efforts to get the right type of youth in the movement and that to train them adequately was still more difficult. I also found to my chagrin that the host of other leaders who surrounded Netaji led a double life. They appeared in public flaunting khadi shirt and *dhoti* or *pyjamas*, while they otherwise moved about in western attire and aped the British in drinking, and clubbing. Altogether this only served to confuse me further. This confusion was also bolstered by my earlier experience during the A.I.C.C. session which was held at Patna. Most of the notables had stayed at the residence of Dr. Sachchidanand Sinha, where we used to meet regularly. It was a motley crowd, westernized and affluent, yet advocating the Indian style of living and spitting fire in support of the poor. I found the exception in the case of Mahatmaji, who appeared to be one with the poor from all angles, and also Lala Lajpat Rai. His simple style of living, betokened a native of the soil, and not a sophisticated and insincere anglophile, which the others appeared to be.

The fear of authority was an important factor then. While in college a delegation of senior students, waited on the Principal to convince him of the unsuitability of holding periodical tests which were no part of the assessment and overall worth of the students. I was part of a delegation of about thirty students—including several friends who obtained positions later in the senior civil service of the country. As we argued the point, with myself located in the front rank, I had the mortification of seeing the other members of the delegation melt away as they sensed the indignation of the Principal. This Principal could help students obtain appropriate positions in the government hierarchy, including posts of teachers in the college and these were scarce and difficult to get. Ultimately I was left as the lone arguer and was faced with the threat of rustication from college even though I was the recipient of the highest scholarship award for merit. The students were in no mood to face authority even though they felt that theirs was a right cause.

It was about this time that I had a glimpse of the pathetic plight of the police Constable. Cycling around, I was taking a short cut at a traffic island. I was faced by a traffic Sub-Inspector. This resulted in a *chalan* against me in the local court. The police Constable, who came to serve the notice at our house, looked forward to a *bakshish* possibly for reporting that the person concerned was not traced ! Thereafter perhaps no trace of the reports would have been found and the matter would end. Perhaps the checking officer may have laid no complaint if he had been approached in the proper manner with the usual fees. It was clear that the police Constables were in the grip of a vice, with their seniors forming one end and their own family commitments being at the other end. Their monthly salaries were in a single figure only and were quite inadequate to make both ends meet. I had to visit the police court office as a sequel to this episode. I was advised to admit the charge so that the matter could be disposed of quickly. Considering that there was no traffic sign displayed, I could contest the charge but this would have meant several visits to the court and perhaps also a lawyer's assistance. Having accepted my fault, I was asked to pay a princely fine of forty-five rupees for this petty offence, if this could be designated as such. I discovered then how devious the procedure really was. An ex-librarian of the Patna Science College, who got a place in the Provincial Executive Service, was a witness to the court proceedings in which I was awarded the fine. He was helpful and arranged to depute a chaprasi to go with me from counter to counter so that I could deposit the fine-money and be allowed to get away from the court. At the end of it all the chaprasis also expected a tip for the help rendered ! I found there several police Constables in the queue waiting to receive cash for which they would affix their thumb-impression on the acquittance roll. I noticed their barracks in close vicinity of the court office, which could hardly be distinguished from hovels. It was clear that the mass of illiterate Constables was merely to act as the strong arm of junior police formations to enforce the will of the government. Their living conditions were wretched and they enjoyed little respect in the governmental hierarchy. They could make illegal gains, which was connived at by their seniors. The British officers had nothing but disdain for them but outwardly bestowed paternal care over their individual difficulties. As for the effective subordinate of the middle rung, he gave the impression of being a tough and ill mannered desperado, submissive only to the superiors in his service. Both the subordinates and the middle ranks had an unattractive banner of duty, but those in the higher echelons could help the common man and their own departmental subordinates. They appeared to be operating the entire governmental machine with the C.I.D in their pockets and thus provided an appropriate avenue of training for keeping the power edifice. An assignment in the police department, in the higher ranks which had been thrown open to Indians, therefore appeared sufficiently attractive to me. The prospects were also attractive from the point of view of financial implications and the position enjoyed in the social frame. There was another opening available for Indians, though the number was extremely limited, of entry into the police at the level of the provincial gazetted service. However, the place in the scale of seniority provided for them was such as to make their jobs unattractive at least for those who could take the open competitive test for the Indian Police Service. I felt therefore that I should take my chance for the I.P. examination. The challenges were mainly of the red tape-officiousness and corruption bordering on oppression. These needed to be contended with and I wanted to play a part in it. Another point which tipped the balance in favour of the police, was the extremely limited opening in the commissioned ranks of the army. Here the chances of promotion of Indian officers were very poor and they appeared powerless in helping the common man. The position in the police was much better.

2

THE INDIAN POLICE

PROVINCIAL autonomy came in 1937 under arrangements made by Government for the gradual transfer of authority and power. This resulted in the formation of ministries in each province, responsible generally to the Legislative Assembly of the province. Important departments including the Police which was the sole instrument of general governance, however, remained under the direct control of provincial Governors. Appointments to the Indian Police were made by the Secretary of State for India on the basis of examinations held in the country, and the interviews for selection were arranged in provincial groups in which this service was divided and cadred. It was quite on the cards that the provincial Chief Minister, who was now on the Interview Board, would throw his weight in for candidates who were resident of the province and possibly his own caste-men. This was greatly disappointing and it appeared that when independence came our way it would probably usher in an era of rule of the locals and inter-provincial rivalries may develop on much the same lines as the north-south difference in the early years of the United States of America. The earlier government had adopted the domicile rules virtually confining government employment in each province to the sons of the soil. But I had hoped that in the Imperial service these considerations would not arise. This hope was negatived. It was apparent that sons of the soil would be awarded high marks in the interview, so that the others would virtually be barred from success. So, that was the style and the entry into the service appeared to be unedifying. Yet the alternatives were either to serve the country through the Servants of the People Society of Lala Lajpat Rai or the Servants of India Society of Gokhale. Both these avenues did not appear as attractive. These points also counted with me in my decision to take the examination for selection to the Indian Police. Though disapproved of by the Congress leaders, even the scions of their families were putting in applications for this service. Sons of important Congress leaders also took the examination with me. I appeared for the interview in the year 1938 when the Board consisted of foreigners only except for Sir Shafat Ahmed Khan of Allahabad University, who was a member of the then Federal Public Services Commission, and the provincial Chief Minister. In spite of the difficulties and impediments, I was successful in the first try. I was the recipient of messages of congratulation from all our relatives, friends, and acquaintances. Even the newspapers considered it fit to carry this news in fairly bold headlines. That a non-native of the province had been taken in the job was not too happy tidings to many of the educated elite in Patna, who wanted that only locals, which meant their own castemen or relatives, should come up. The views expressed by Rai Bahadur Shyam Nandan Sahay, a landlord from Muzaffarpur, later to become the Vice Chancellor of Patna University and also a member of the Council of States at Delhi (a forum of senior politicians) was that he was looking forward to enjoying the breeze under a banyan tree in the compound of my residence, where I would be posted. The senior police officers enjoyed special privileges and all callers at their residences, specially the natives, had to cool their heels in such abject comfort before being ushered into the presence of those in power.

I was directed to join the Police Training Institution at Hazaribagh. This training was indeed an eye opener, showing to me the postures to be adopted for ruling your own people. I had looked forward to some grilling. But suprises awaited me. The instructors in the Institution were of the non-gazetted ranks, and felt humble before us, as the possibility of being posted under us in later years was not unlikely. Unlike the accepted procedures at Sandhurst or other training institutions for the army in England, we were "sirred" on the parade ground and the riding school. A similar picture prevailed even in the sports field, and taking part in sports was compulsory. It was interesting that the British counterparts in the service, who were placed for training with me—I was the only Indian—were very hostile and critical of everything Indian. They were suspicious of the Indian elements in the police including myself and the Principal of the institution, who was a senior Britisher straightway ruled that while under training I should fall in line with the young trainees drawn from U.K. particularly in the style of living and the daily chores. We lived in the I.P. Mess and had to dress for dinner in the old time dinner jacket and stiff front shirt. The boys from England were not accustomed to this routine either but had been schooled in this before I joined them. We were expected to mix socially mainly with the local foreigners and perhaps a few Indians who were considered to be pronouncedly pro-government. Even a visit to the local cinema hall dressed in a lounge suit evoked an order of confinement to the Police Mess building for a week. Apparently we should not have been seen in the evening in public places of amusement or entertainment except in formal attire. Severer notice was taken of the truancy of one of my British counterparts, who had the temerity to go out on his push bike to enjoy the fun in the bazar on the occasion of Holi. Even our food habits were sought to be changed to suit the colonial requirements. We had to learn to depend a lot on imported tinned food and to imbibe liquor. The Principal of the institution was fond of the bottle himself and his monthly bills at the clubs ran into four figures, nearly gobbling up his entire salary. This was a poor prospect as I had been trained to a life of moderation and simple living. The hauteur of my British counterparts was galling particularly in view of the looming prospect of greater political autonomy. The Indians by and large were getting out of the era of inferiority complex vis-a-vis the rulers, matching their wits with them in all fields of activity. I found, for example, that within a month of joining the training centre, I could pass all the examinations while the incumbents imported from England lagged far behind. Also relevant was the fact that one of the trainees was the scion of a British Warrant Officer, who had seen service in the N.W.F.P. and had had part of his schooling in the famous *Ghora Gali* which was the centre for the education of such second class British employees in India. His I.Q. was not particularly high and even in the much vaunted field of sports including riding, which required a certain amount of dash, his performance could not even match the cadets training for Sub-Inspectorship or the provincial police service, Deputy Superintendent of Police.

The training included education in criminal law and procedure, proficiency in the local language, work on the parade ground, and visits to trial courts and police offices of various denominations.

As I had got through all the tests early, the balance of the year was utilised by me in studying other local languages like Oriya,—the province of Orissa then formed part of the cadre area to be covered by us—and Mundari, the language of the tribals in Ranchi area. I attempted to probe the ideas of the Britisher under training on problems with which we were concerned. It surprised me to see how casual their consideration for local matters was. I started studying the Ramayana even though my knowledge of the Hindi language was extremely poor, having studied Urdu and Persian during my school and college days. This was viewed with disfavour by my Principal, who felt that I could fruitfully study the Bible. I paid more than one visit to the Sunday service of the local church and this appeared to have enthused him greatly.

This training in narrow grooves dismayed me and I could not understand why the incumbents in each area were trained separately. The idea was to avoid over centralisation as I realised later. And it was indeed very thoughtful. The training was merely to orient the young officer to the conditions of the country and no specialisation was intended as superior police work was counted as the sphere of the generalist. Therefore the standard of training for police work proper was not much different than what would be appropriate to a Sergeant. There was no study of criminology, criminal investigation, or even higher administrative procedures. All that was needed was to create a feeling of superiority whereby subjective justice to the subordinates, would be ensured and they alone had primarily to keep the administration going. This impartiality no provincial service was capable of providing. And on this point some doubts were creeping up in the case of the Indian police officers as well particularly the Indian incumbents because of the peculiar recruitment procedures in which local patriotism and wirepulling appeared to play an important part.

After arrival at Hazaribagh to join the training college, I went to the room of the Superintendent of the college, a Deputy Superintendent of Police promoted from the rank of Sub-Inspector. I attempted to rest on the table while talking to this officer, but he promptly reminded me that the table was to be used for keeping records and papers. He advised that I should occupy the chair and in the service it would generally be at the head of the table. He also inculcated the principle that a subordinate officer should take his seat only after he had been permitted to do so. This was a matter of discipline, and a must for the police department.

As a new officer under training, I had to take up the distribution of pay of Sub Inspector cadets. This was done in typical army style, with the cashier standing by with the cash and the candidates marching up one by one, to receive the money, appending their signatures on the rolls and then marching back to their seats. In the case of other subordinates like the orderlies, they invariably affixed their thumb impression as most of them were illiterate and were recruited mainly because of their association or relationship with some other policemen. It was a surprise to me, on completing the pay disbursal, that there was a shortage of a hundred rupees in the available cash. Apparently some of these officers had received extra money but nobody was prepared to own it. The shortage had to be made good by me from my personal funds. I had the foretaste of what I was in for, the service was to be a game in which there should be checks and counterchecks and little honesty could be expected from the subordinates which included the Sub-Inspectors ! A short course in Survey and Settlement operations was given to us as a considerable amount of the policeman's time was expected to be spent in solving the confrontations due to land disputes, which even erupted into violent riots. Sometimes serious situations could develop and could take the complexion of dacoity and maraudery. Little interest was taken by us in the Survey training as it appeared that we would have competent help from subordinates. All we needed to know were a few technical terms so that we could appreciate the content of a complaint. The examination, which came at the end of this period of training, was typical of the kind of work we might be required to take up later. The subordinates, who earlier acted as instructors and were now invigilators in the test, were only too happy to help us answer the questions. The result was a cent per cent pass. During Survey and Settlement training, I was dismayed to find a clear stratification of the trainees i.e. the superior Indian element keeping to themselves while the Britishers preferred to form their own group. The provincial service personnel, who also joined the training course conjointly with the Imperial service members, appeared to jostle with each other to gain admittance to the tents allotted to the *Sahibs*, perhaps to curry favour with them. This showed servility of the highest order. The provincial services were in fact officered by people of this type so as to enable the senior foreigners to function more effectively with an elan that could be developed only in a group of sycophants and "yes-sirs". This resulted in an attitude of disdain which constituted one of the pillars of British discipline in India. The loyalty and obedience of the subordinates was an accepted position and this was born of sycophancy and a desire to get on. This was achievable by such conduct.

The level of corruption in the administration was brought vividly before us by our Instructor in Survey and Settlement work, a senior officer of the Provincial Civil Service. A few years earlier he had been posted as a junior Deputy Collector in Hazaribagh when a notable shikari, who had bagged a man-eater, was given a reward of rupees five hundred by government. Months later the shikari stood at the porch of the Deputy Commissioner's office, to greet him when he was to leave office. This I.C.S. officer was pleased to see the shikari and enquired of his welfare. However, the shikari brought out a hundred rupee note from his pocket and publicly presented it to the Deputy Commissioner. This officer was non-plussed and wanted to know what it all was about and in any case an explanation for this audacity was required. The shikari undeterred reported that he was left with only a hundred rupee currency note out of the reward money given to him and he had brought it for the D.C. as he thought this must be his share of the reward ! The D.C. could do nothing about it. Corruption had become a routine of governmental work and it appeared to cause no revulsion among the people. Only when it was collected under duress or threat of positive harm or when vivid and palpable injustice was done by a law court did people feel that notice should be taken of it. The common Hindustani proverb *Jab Mian Beevi Razi to Kya Karega Qazi* could not be apter for such deals. Corruption was a matter between two parties and was condoned and glossed over. It was to assume other hues soon after.

In September, 1939, war was officially declared and India was embroiled in it as she was a part of the British Empire. Two British I. C. S. officers were undergoing training with us at Hazaribagh, and were in the age-bracket for being drafted into the armed forces specially as one of them was also a trained pilot. Both were the objects of much sympathy as in India, away from the field of war, they were safe and yet on the pedestals of authority keeping the Empire going. However, to me it meant one step nearer the goal of the country's independence. I looked forward to playing an important role, once independence was achieved. The general impression was that the politicians, drawn generally from the back benches in the colleges and professions in active life, would need the full assistance of the more capable civil servants. The prospect was quite interesting but events were to show how very mistaken my idea was.

During training we made a trip to an old sentry post on a hill-top about fifteen miles from Hazaribagh. It intrigued us as to why this hill-top post was set up by the earlier administrators of the East India Company's regime. Apparently these were posts for occupation-forces which terrorised the people in villages round it and kept a look out for any concerted movement Shackles such as these of the country's slavery were forged by the forces of the administration but nearly a hundred years of organised alien administration had rendered this unnecessary. The country was now culturally and financially completely dominated. The ruined state of the hill-top post bore eloquent testimony to this. The shackles which bound the country now were the new thesis of life with emphasis on visible power and not the inner strength which had distinguished the country. In short, the slave mentality had been fully implanted and moral standards had degenerated.

We had a foretaste of the new technique of teargas here. This was experimented within our own institution building. Considering that the type of teargas to be used had not been finalised, the experiment appeared very impressive. The after affects lasted quite some time even though we were exposed to the smoke for but a brief period of time. It was not before independence was achieved and in fact several years later that tear smoke squibs started being used against recalcitrant crowds, but these were found incapable of doing the trick, what with wind directions and the dispersal of gas in open areas. I was dismayed to find that there were no other attempts at catching up with scientific developments which had come up the world over.

Another interesting episode which clings to my mind relates to an Anglo Indian Deputy Superintendent of Police. This official's original British forebear was perhaps in the fourth generation but such was his emotional attraction to England that he informed us when we visited his office that his home was actually in Kent and not in India. He made the interesting assertion that he was not making any visit to U.K. as he may not like to return to this alien land, where his family had amassed a pretty large fortune. There were several others of this variety, one a functionary of the local Reformatory School for juvenile delinquents, who was always on the alert to inveigle young boys from England to his home in the vain hope that they might fall for the young ladies in the houschold. Incidentally one of these young girls had earned the unenviable title of man-eater of young men only.

At the end of the training, I found that I had little grasp of the job that would present itself before me. But with the machinery running and letting things take their predetermined course, little difficulty was expected in accomplishing the task ahead. As noted by me earlier also, considering that the police administrator was a generalist, not really interested in the technical chores of the field-officer, the training given was admirable although some study of police lore including interesting investigative procedures would have been appropriate. The disciplinary aspect of the worse worried me. I realised that the emerging political leadership in the country had great concern for the subordinates, but the reasons for it were not so much consideration for the underdog as the desire to help their own kith and kin. Almost the entire leadership had connections at the lower rungs of the administrative ladder. Therefore the code of discipline had to be less vigorous. I was aware now that the police force with all its facade of unity of purpose, was riven into sections, the result of the feudalistic order which prevailed. I would have to fall in line with the local kulak group, as I had no moorings of my own. In any case the British elements preferred to be left alone, counting the days of their liquidation. Absence of local links, would enable me to act with the Britisher's balance and yet I had sympathy for my junior colleagues, which I felt would make me more effective and useful. The local breed of senior officers could not equal this situation.

I proceeded to Patna to continue my period of probation, to learn and also to effectively perform police functions. An important publication in the newspapers those days was the excerpts from the official Gazette, reporting the posting of senior officers. While the names of those in the two Imperial services, the I.C.S. and the I.P. were prefixed with the honorific Mister (Mr), those in the other services, however senior, were designated as Babu, *Maulvi* or Sardar. This distinction gave a kick to the ego of the Indian members of the Imperial services. These distinctions were abolished after the country attained independence in 1947, when all were designated as "Shri." In regard to the award of titles and honours, this position was similar as the non-imperial service incumbents could look forward to titles like Rai Bahadur, Raja Bahadur, and so on, but the Imperial service holders were decorated with knighthood, or C.I.E. or O.B.E. and so on. There was even distinction in regard to travel concessions. While we were required to travel first class by trains even if not on duty, government would pay allowance for journeys on duty, the other services could only attain this standard after they had received a level of emoluments which few among them could aspire to. The Director of Veterinary Services, for example, whose maximum salary was of the order of about a thousand rupees per month, had to content himself by travelling only second class. He was normally not accommodated in the Circuit House provided at the headquarters of each district. And this was also the close preserve of the Imperial services. All these distinctions made me feel important and to some extent self conscious. In any case it did not conduce to my doing better in the Police Service.

3

OFFICER UNDER TRAINING

As was the vogue, I was appointed substantively to the Indian Police immediately after completing my training, having passed all the examinations. However, a certain amount of training in office routine was yet to be completed and this was to go hand in hand with normal work in the field as well. Soon I was faced with the stern realities of this life. The senior officers under whom I was to get trained, worked in narrow grooves with a strong caste and provincial bias. An interesting function, a horse racing meet, was arranged in the local maidan early in the new year. It had the attendant details, the paddock, tote, and all. The provincial Governor honoured us with his presence. However, it was sad to see senior police officers busying themselves either in calculating their chances on the tote or hovering around the Governor and his entourage with a view to catching the Governor's eye. The result was a complete melee the responsibility for which was fastened by the top brass on the local managers of the meet. Soon I was to realise that the normal system of functioning in the department was the railway train system in which the engine's impact was passed on to the last bogie. The senior officers found it convenient to pass the buck down the line, looking for scapegoats. And even in this hunt, the unattached subordinates got the rub while co-castemen and relations got away without any adverse remarks. Then followed an interesting incident in which a bicycle was involved in a minor collision with a rickshaw. When the cyclist and the rickshaw-wala came to the police station to record their complaint, it was found that both of them wanted to make it up with each other. As no injury worth the name had been caused to either party, an entry was recorded under my orders at the police station, where I was training. The remarks from the senior formations, showed that this procedure was highly improper and that the parties should have been sent to the court. This simple affair would have resulted in a long drawn out wrangle with considerable ill-feeling between the two groups and waste of time and money for both. Such remarks were not understood by me. It appeared that all this was the result of a plan to put officers not belonging to the proper bracket in the wrong box. Encomiums were reserved only for the people of one's own group. The lower ranks in the police, however, showed a surprising understanding of this position. Though poor in technical training, and with little education in the mechanics of their work, they were entirely loyal, and not inclined to get involved in the caste racket. The constabulary with hardly any education, presented a spectacle of loyalty of a higher order and that was the principal attraction of the force.

During the course of my normal duties I had to check various types of transport on the road and finding one of the cab drivers at fault, I sent a report against him to the local court. In the days after independence, such cases would come up in the courts for hearing years later, but the position was then so amazingly good that within a few months the driver was summoned to the court to stand trial. I had to appear as the principal prosecution witness. The trying court was an honorary Magistrate, who was a title holder, a landlord, and *rais*. Rather than place me in the witness box, he gave me a seat on the dias, but the lawyer for the accused raised a serious objection and wanted that I should be placed in the proper enclosure. This was appropriate, but the honorary Magistrate, did not allow this and ruled that the place where I was given the seat should be considered as a part of the witness box. The defence lawyer wanted to make out a story that the prosecution was based on personal animus and that the driver had refused to serve as my personal car driver and hence this trumped up charge. This was done to irritate me so that I might make some disparaging remarks about the accused which would give the lawyer a handle to tell the Magistrate that I was biased. Already he had showed off to his client by asking me to be treated as a common witness. Before I could object to such tendentious accusations hurled by the lawyer, the court came into the picture and warned the lawyer that the quantum of fine to be imposed on his client was mounting as he had started raising at random points and putting insulting questions. This unnerved the lawyer and even the accused begged for pardon, stating that he had not met me earlier and it was the lawyer who had persuaded him to put up this defence. A heavy fine was imposed and also a sentence for imprisonment was awarded in default. I was agreeably surprised at the cooperative attitude of the Magistrate and was happy at the consideration that he gave to me. The honorary Magistrate had seen through the game and knew what the defence was up to. The rationale of the system of honorary Magistrate was quick justice and in a manner in which justice was not only dispensed but appeared to be so. The people in general fully understood this and were appreciative of it all. The system has been given up now due to the corruption that crept into its fold consequent on politicisation of the assignments.

I was appalled at the poor condition of the office where I worked and in particular the accommodation, and furniture. I had expected things to be much better. And the whip hand the clerks had in transacting business, was extremely disappointing. We had a bespectacled clerk (*moharrir*), who sported his caste-mark prominently, as the scribe in charge of the crime section. He appeared to be the de-facto controller of all investigations and recorded comments freely on the investigational papers. These were meekly signed by the police officers presiding over the section. There was no doubt that the officers lacked proper insight into crime papers and were loath to strive to attain mastery over the matter, which the *moharrir* possessed. It was no surprise to find that in the New Year honours list, this clerk was raised to the pedestal of a Raisahebship. It was a decade later that I learnt of the story of a very senior police officer in Rajasthan, possibly having risen from the ranks, who was requested to approve of a draft letter in a file. This officer reportedly turned round and swore at the clerk for his naivete as a superior police officer was expected to sign orders and not scrutinize drafts, which job was well within the domain of work of ministerial subordinates. The erudite Head-*moharrir* of the Patna Police Office also passed the final orders, which were signed on the dotted line by the officers concerned.

The impression which I had carried about the senior Indian police officers being near the centre of power, was a mistaken one. The Indian part of the cadre consisted of a small fraction of those promoted from the provincial services. The conditions of service of these officers were so framed as to make of them a pack of position and promotion hunters, prepared to sell their souls to the ruling elements. This group caused differences in the rank of directly recruited Indian police officers as well. The result was that the senior ranks of Indian officers were completely disunited. The non-Indian elements kept together, and exercised all the influence over the top formations. I was also horrified to find no understanding of the problems particularly those which concerned personnel matters. The staff used for this work was ill-educated and completely incompetent. The custom was merely to hark back to precedents framed by senior British elements and even to the extent of hair splitting with regard to these orders. There was no attempt to formulate new methods, for which there was a real need.

As a junior member of the Indian Police posted to the headquarters station of the metropolitan district, I was always placed in command of the parade which was rigged up on the occasion of the formal visit of the Deputy Inspector General of the Range or the Inspector General. Other luminaries were not expected to make such visits. On such occasions all the officers had to pay compliments to the chief in full regalia, which included riding boots and spurs. We carried swords whose blades were brandished only on the parade ground. Otherwise a hand salute had to be exchanged. The parade was by no means numerically large and the turn-out of the officers and the men left much to be desired. I felt extremely unhappy about this. But there were its humorous aspects as well. The D.I.G. then was of generous proportions who found it difficult to buy a Sam-Browne belt to fit his girth. He would like the parade to be a quick affair as he naturally found his legs too slender to take the load of the frame. He revelled in making remarks in a microscopic hand : apparently he expected that all this would go unread. The parade and inspection work was a formality and the important part was the intervening social get-togethers with beer sessions that kept every one in good humour. A cursory glance at office-papers was adequate and the mid-day siesta helped in expediting disposal of the work. The government was kept going by a show of power and not by scrutinising details, which would in any case take care of themselves. The office papers were best looked after by clerks and could not orders be framed either way, to support or oppose a particular individual ? What did it matter if in a few cases, some people were sent up on charges which appeared to be not fully substantiated ? The dictum was, "Wait and see, and act when you must".

Gambling, essentially a social ill, was construed as constituting an important factor of crime causation. Though not entitled to issue any warrants, the District Superintendent of Police was empowered to issue search warrants for premises suspected to be used for gaming. And about the time of the annual Diwali celebrations there appeared to be a complete craze for gambling with even some private residences being rigged up for this item of entertainment. Naturally it brought gains to the landlord. These circumstances fulfilled the requirements of the law in regard to the common gaming house set-up, and this was actionable. The Deputy Superintendent of Police in Patna had some information about some such gambling dens in the township. He promptly obtained the Superintendent of Police's warrant and sent the informant, a police Sub-Inspector, along with a body of the Constables attached to the police station on an *ekka*—police transport was not motorised then. The Deputy Superintendent followed them in his car and I was directed to accompany him as an item of my training. As we reached the neighbourhood, the posse of policemen effected entrance in the house, without observing any legal formalities. The persons inside the house were taken in custody and arraigned for gambling. I was amused to find some constables pull out a pack of cards from the roof of the house and this was termed as the vehicle for the gaming exercise. The persons in the house had some money on their person and this was also seized as the amount which was intended to be used for gambling. The Deputy Superintendent was gleeful and thought he had made a good haul. The manner in which the raid was effected and the evidence which was sought to be foisted on the arrested persons to prove their guilt, amused me greatly. This was the peculiar style of police work, which revelled in building a case on the evidence of a few others who were allowed to get away though involved in a crime or supposed crime and were cited as witnesses to the episode in the court. I learnt later that the persons arrested were local rowdies and had perhaps got together to have a drink. There could not be a better opportunity of nabbing them and the charge of gambling was easy to establish ! This was padding par excellence and even senior echelons appeared to fall in line with their subordinates in this work. Items such as this made the police dreaded in the State. The way the official search and seizure lists were prepared to conform to the law, was a spectacle which did not add to the stature of the police in the mind of a young police officer such as me. I learnt that a good part of the money seized was siphoned off by not including it in the seizure list. No complaint on this point was launched as the arrested persons hoped thereby to be treated lightly.

As part of my training, I was seconded to a police station. Here, I was also required to go out for night patrol. The whole system was oriented for an illiterate staff. The men were provided with one, two, and three hole discs which were required to be hung up at appropriate places once every two hours, in a six-hourly beat of duty. In between the beat Constable was also given static duty. Three Constables thus formed a group and performed patrol in two hourly beats. Even middle rung inspecting officers were expected to hang up discs at the points checked in token of doing the work! It was embarrassing to get along on a car at night stopping at specified points to check how the patrol was going, only to find the men in a state of utter disarray. On many occasions the turban of the beat Constable found asleep at his post of static watch, was removed and he was charged the next day with dereliction of duty. Quite numerous were the occasions on which the Constables were discovered going about clad in dhotis. These defaulters were normally paraded before the Inspector the next morning. Some of them were consigned to the orderly room in the Lines for punishment drill. The major domo of these parades was the Sergeant Major, who was generally drawn from the rank of N.C.O. of a British Regiment. The Sergeant Major enjoyed the complete confidence of the District Superintendent and was the de-facto boss to whom the constabulary in the Lines and outside looked up to for rewards and condign punishment. On one occasion when I proceeded to attend the orderly room, I was astounded to find the Sergeant Major busy with the Indian Superintendent of Police, quite oblivious of the comings and goings of other officers. He failed to rise from the seat on my arrival or pay the usual compliments. When I complained to the S.P. regarding the impropriety, I was informed that the Sergeant Major should be left severely alone as he enjoyed the confidence of the higher British officers. Such improprieties and complete lack of decorum at the hands of British subordinates, had to be tolerated by the Indian officers. This exhibition of subservience was galling to me. I felt like resigning from the service when such monstrous conduct had to be condoned. But my college teachers, who had earlier considered that I was cut out for a professorial assignment, advised me to carry on in the new job, in which they felt that I could bring about some changes for the better, despite difficulties. The position was indeed full of contradictions.

A good part of police work was conducted in secret and confidential sections of the office. The 'X' Branch of the S.P.'s office was an important section and was generally in the hands of Anglo-Indian assistants. Junior Indian officers like me were not taken into confidence regarding the details of working of this section. The idea was that we would learn all about it in the course of the day-to-day work. Another idea was to involve the smallest fraction of officers and specially the Indian elements who had to be watched before being allowed in the inner sanctum. Even the confidential reports on the work of subordinate officers of the department were kept away and no instruction or advice regarding their maintenance was available. I was also attached to an Inspector of Police for learning investigation work. When the Inspector made some comments on the case-records prepared by me, he was told to expunge them and was required merely to convey the gist of instructions to me personally. The work of senior officers indeed was not to be commented on by mere underlings, particularly where native subordinates were concerned vis-a-vis non-Indian seniors.

The sloppy turn out of the average policeman was a constant item of ridicule and his behaviour specially the local habit of chewing tobacco (known as *khaini*) was the subject matter of skits and burlesque shows both in and out of the departmental forum. The numerical insufficiency of policemen was also patent. Their training left much to be desired. The leadership was provided by half-baked foreign elements and the caste-ridden local elite. Corruption involving collection of regular imposts was the order of the day. It was shocking to learn soon after I joined duty that night patrol Constables from one of the patrolling centres known as a town outpost, had gone out to collect Dussehra tolls, and this exercise included a retired senior Deputy Collector's residence. The toll was attempted to be collected in the presence of the local police chief, who went unrecognised by the errant police Constable. Having been called on to conduct the official enquiry known as departmental proceedings against this Constable, I had to take down the evidence of the retired Deputy Collector. This gentleman regaled me with stories about the peons (*chaprassis*) attached to the Divisional Commissioners of his days. On one occasion, the chaprassi called on him along with the Commissioner's cook, designated as the *khansama*. They asked for the *salami* i.e. the fee for paying the official call. This Deputy Collector was not one of the common run of Indian officers recruited in the provincial service and had on his own toured round various parts of the world—very unusual for a provincial service man. He declined to make the usual presents, but to his mortification the cook arranged to put the Divisional Commissioner in a frenzy the very next morning by not making appropriate arrangements for his tea and breakfast. This deficiency was placed entirely at the doors of the Deputy Collector, who was alleged to have hurled insulting remarks on the Commissioner, and had refused to help the servant in procuring the ingredients for the meals. Despite all the protests that he could make, the result was a bad chit in the character-roll of this officer from the Commissioner. This militated against his future promotion. Apparently irregular and corrupt practices like this were encouraged and connived at by senior officers. Two years later when I got posted as a District S.P. in the province of Orissa, I had the mortification of finding that even the I.G. Police on his tour to my District specially commissioned a junior policeman of the rank of Inspector to arrange for huge quantities of grocery, vegetables etc. for his personal consumption. And the Inspector had the temerity of obtaining the stuff by railway parcel from distant Bangalore. He was apparently showing his fine taste to the police chief. The police chief also accepted this lot of things and paid a pittance without batting an eyelid. Apparently even senior officers did not object to such hospitality as long as it did not concern the *izzat* of the Raj. I also learnt to my utter mortification that an ex-District Police Superintendent had most of his salary impounded because of his earlier escapades including a divorce. But he could still manage to carry on as the supplies for his daily consumption were made by local landlords under the full blare of official intelligence.

Senior police officers of gazetted rank were expected to supervise personally the investigation of the more interesting or serious offences. The detailed investigation in any case, was the responsibility of the subordinate investigator. Hence the epithet that the subordinate police were the real arbiters of the fate of complaints about crimes. A police officer of the rank of Sub-Inspector would take in hand the investigation of all cognizable cases of his area, whatever their degree of importance. The evidence initially recorded by him in the diaries was what mattered. Supervision by senior officers was only a mild brake on their cupidity in the compilation of evidence. It is this class of police officers who had to get together the witnesses for examination by his superiors for supervision of the cases ; and in the process the witnesses could easily be tutored or monitored. I was required to supervise a case of burglary in the house of a local Executive Engineer which had some interesting facets. This officer, a Pathan from western Punjab, knew my father, as he also belonged to the Public Works Department. This was one reason I was detailed for this work. The midnight intruder was picking up items from the bedroom when the engineer was roused and reportedly challenged him. The criminal then made good his escape with the booty and he could not be caught. I was surprised to find that even though the engineer saw the culprit, who wore no mask, he could give no details of the man. It was also found that he had a loaded revolver under his pillow but there was no indication of it having been used. My enquiries indicated that having switched on the electric light, the Pathan engineer finding the burglar busy in his bedroom, pulled out the revolver, but did not have the strength to pull the trigger and was too nervous to shout for help. He also remembered not a whit of the particulars of the culprit. The incident showed to me the infirmities of the educated Indian, who was quite incapable of defending himself. It also made clear the difficulty of investigation by the police when no clue whatsoever was available in most cases. Without any details of items stolen or any indication about the identification particulars of culprits, the possibility of detection, was very slim indeed. I found that only about ten per cent of the cases of house breaking could be detected and in most of these the culprits were local and by mischance had been caught in the act of committing these crimes. There was no indication of any investigative expertise being brought in by the police in these cases.

The ceremonial part of police work was, however, very attractive. I was extended an invitation to the functions to which my father got the summons only at a late stage in his official career. This privilege was denied to provincial service officers except the very senior ones. The same was the case with the annual police parade, which was a glittering show and was presided over by the Governor of the province. His arrival at the parade ground with all the trappings of office including the entourage of ADCs caused considerable flutter in the social dovecotes and the audience which collected to witness the *tamasha* was indeed a large one. I had a small part to play in it being yet a junior officer but I could see that the entire Indian audience took pride in having been invited to the show. I felt indeed proud to be in it. These shows were given up during the period of the War, which had already been declared towards the end of 1939. After independence, the parade ritual continued but it lacked the lustre of the previous shows. There were no Darbars in the Governor's residence.

An interesting episode in regard to the observance of Moharram, in the district is worth recounting. As part of my training I was deputed to a nearby township where in the past Moharram processions had come to loggerheads over a question of precedence. Sometimes the clash was with Hindus on the question of getting across a *peepal* tree fallen on the route. Some branches of the *peepal* tree would normally have to be lopped off to allow the Moharram flags to be carried forward. But it may have been easier to dig down the passage so that the sentiments of the Hindus were not touched by lopping of branches of the sacred tree and the Moharram banners could also pass by. A small body of armed policemen was also detailed with me and it was my special job to oversee their work. It was considered that armed men could be led impartially by officers of the senior service, specially in sensitive areas where clashes were likely to take place. It was also customary to post a Magistrate with this force and only under his instructions could firing be resorted to, if necessary. The armed unit was, however, under the supervisory control of the senior police officer. There was thus a system of dual control in which both the magistracy and the police had to function as the twin limbs of administration supplementing each other and neither could act independently. However, the police had the upper hand as in certain contingencies, the Magistrate could be bypassed and the orders of firing could be given by the senior police officer himself. The Magistrate, who was posted with me, belonged to the provincial service and had had a large number of years in government employ. He fully realised that he had merely to act as an aide to me and was to issue instructions for firing as and when required to do so by me. As the deputation lasted for well over a week, during which period the Moharram processions were taken out daily, my job was to see that the armed policemen were fit and fine and that the local police were active and kept me informed of the safe conduct of processions. In effect they saw to everything and merely reported on two or three occasions during the day about the peace that prevailed. They made it clear to me that it was not necessary to make a show of force, which indeed may be like the proverbial red rag to the bull. The Magistrate also bemused himself by studying some of his office records and particularly of the cases tried by him. Magistrates had both executive and judicial functions. And finally when the main day of the procession was over and merely the backlash would continue for another two days, he quietly informed me that it was needless for me to waste time there. He said that I could safely go back to my headquarters. This was incorrect advice as the armed party would continue to be stationed there for the next two days also. Being yet inexperienced and ill-advised by the subordinate Magistrate I returned to my headquarters before the due date. The episode indicated that the police was a working machine which required little additional effort to run it and the magistracy, legally the authority to exercise discretion in the matter of law and order, was resigned to pander to the plans of the police force, which indeed was the effective ruling machine with little to do. I was at a lose end and toyed with the idea of making amendments in the police drill which appeared too mechanical and somewhat comical. I could not understand the import of the movements on the parade ground, which were unsuitable for police work. Yet I found that this was an exercise in futility. It was only necessary to develop a parental attitude towards the mass of the force particularly of the armed wing, so that their loyalty was assured. The common man, like the soldier in the army, was used to whimsical leadership provided by the luminaries of the predecessor

Mughal dispensation. The Britishers had greatly followed this pattern. Therefore, in the police, it was alright if the seniors appeared to be whimsical and this trait made them loved and liked. It was not necessary to embark on any correctives or reforms.

While under training, I paid a visit to distant Punjab and exchanged notes with the younger officers there. The undivided Punjab of the pre-independence period had a reputation for efficiency and severity of control that was the envy of police officers round the country. To my utter chagrin, I learnt that an effective policeman had to have special training in hurling abuse which impressed most of the people. In fact this was looked upon as a necessary adjunct of good administration! The village bully was tamed by harsh and even obscene language sans which he would not be worth his salt. All the same, I was struck to find the utter disgust which the people generally had developed in regard to police officers even though they knuckled down to their style of working.

At the end of a year's period of training, I was posted to Orissa to function as a junior field officer in charge of a sub-division.

4

SUB-DIVISIONAL POLICE OFFICER

THE INDIAN POLICE was administered much on the pattern of the cadre of commissioned officers of the army. The force was divided into commissions, each covering one major province. As the province of Orissa was carved out from Bihar and by adding on some portions of the erstwhile Madras Presidency, all of which had a large proportion of Oriya speaking population, the Indian police cadre for the provinces of Bihar and Orissa continued to be a joint one. Also, the number of posts available in the province of Orissa were so small that these could not sustain a separate cadre. All officers of the Indian police in the Bihar and Orissa cadre had to serve for a period of four to five years in Orissa. For administrative convenience several offices of the province of Orissa, were still located in Bihar notably the office of the Accountant General/ Comptroller was located in Ranchi. Bihar and Orissa, and also the Central Provinces and Berar were pooled into one unit and had a joint Public Services Commission with headquarters at Ranchi. It was because of this arrangement that soon after my training was officially concluded in Bihar, during which period I had a go at several substantive assignments also, that I was shot into the wilderness that was then the new province of Orissa. Another factor which counted was that my father had also then been posted to that province. I had to make the journey to Cuttack, then the provincial capital of Orissa, via Calcutta. Baleshwar Prasad, later to become India's ambassador at Rangoon and also Delhi's Lt. Governor, was then located in Calcutta with a business firm belonging to Rai Bahadur Shyam Nandan Sahay. I was to have stayed with him but as he got a little late in reaching the Howrah railway station the connecting link then was a pontoon bridge which was opened up every night for servicing—I had to go to an hotel as I thought Baleshwar may have gone to Rangoon, a place he frequently visited. During the few hours I was at the hotel, I was struck at the finesse of the white slave traffickers in Calcutta, then considered to be the gayest spot in the east and a city of palaces. Finding a lone young man in the hotel, waiting for his host, the pimps wanted to get round me with prospects of a merry evening. Yet I was agreeably surprised at the hotel management putting me (and perhaps their other clients) wise about the likely approaches which might be made. Going round later with Baleshwar, I found the city effectively policed by constables and sergeants in immaculate white. Most of them were drawn from Bihar and the local Bengalis took to them very kindly. Here no rules of domicile appeared to apply. This made me feel happy indeed : a contrast to the sad position in Bihar. The Bengali was not afraid of any competition from the denizens of other states. Unfortunately these conditions were to change very soon in the face of restrictions being imposed all over the country. I was particularly impressed with the Calcutta traffic police. The expertise the Calcutta police had in crime detection—which included white slave traffic gangsters—was remarkable. The Calcutta police was a name to reckon with in the metropolitan cities of the world. I noted these points in cooperation with my host who had had more experience of this city. I was sure that the police in Orissa would have imbibed some of the good points of the police unit in their neighbourhood. I was specially happy to note the esteem and *izzat* enjoyed by the Commissioner of Police. In the city of Calcutta, it was he who mattered and was placed as number two, counting more or less next to the Governor.

The province of Orissa had only six administrative districts and the three prime conveniences viz., electricity, piped water supply, and an underground sewer system, were not available at any centre. There was no broadcasting station in the province. I was posted as a sub-divisional police officer, to Rayaghada, located on the B.N. railway (Bengal Nagpur railway) link line between Vishakhapatnam (known then as Vizagapatam) and Raipur in C.P. Every sub-division was headed by a civil sub-divisional officer but for police work several sub-divisions did not boast of a gazetted police officer in charge. The sub-division of Rayaghada was very extensive and formed part of the huge district of Koraput, perhaps one of the largest in area in the country. The district was in fact co-terminus with the Jeypore Samasthanam, a Zamindari which in earlier days was the domain of one of the local potentates. This district had a large Oriya speaking population although the upper stratum of the local society was entirely Telugu speaking. Being one of the later acquisitions of the Raj, and having a very large tribal population, the district officer functioned here as a *Mai-Bap* (all in all) on the lines of the dispensation in the country's north west in Punjab, and the North West Frontier Provinces. The District officer in the Punjab and N.W.F.P. areas was styled as Deputy Commissioner and not as District Magistrate and Collector, which was in vogue in the more settled areas in Bengal and Bihar. The district of Koraput in particular sported the designation of the district officer as a Special Agent (to the Governor) and the sub-divisional officer was designated as Special Assistant Agent. These functionaries had wider powers both in revenue and other administrative matters. Perhaps the extensive area, the relative backwardness of the population, and the need for special relations with the estate hierarchy had resulted in Rayaghada subdivision being blessed with the privilege of sporting a sub-divisional police officer as well. It was interesting, however, that the incumbent of this office did not even have a separate office building which functions were performed from a room in the residence, located far away from all human habitations. The sub-divisional officer's residence was located in a reasonably populous sector but not so the police officer's. The idea was that the policeman should stay away from the common crowd. Indeed law and order keeping, though seemingly simple, was a tough job as future events disclosed. In this process of law keeping, the sub-divisional officer, fulfilling some judicial functions also, counted but little. It was the police officer who mattered. It was considered necessary that I should be touring round my area freely, sensing the temper of the tribals and their feelings towards the government. The intelligentsia exploited them to their heart's content and were generally hand in glove with the functionaries of the estate. This was another important point, why a senior policeman was brought into the picture. However, the role of the sub-divisional police officer appeared to be much like that of a Police Inspector. This piqued me greatly. But my idea was to make improvements which an Inspector was not capable of doing.

Perhaps that was the intention of government as well. Thinking on these lines, I started introducing some new procedures for appraising the law and order situation which consisted of compiling statistics and evaluating them in office. All this was mainly concerned with serious crime. This process was a complete departure from the crude charts that were maintained according to rules. However, this beginning had not gathered enough steam when I had a visitor in my office—a foreigner, who I realised later was the District Superintendent of Police. He was passing through Rayaghada and so had called in. He took a look at the graphs and charts that were being put up. But these did not seem to register with him at all. He would rather have no such evaluations as these tended to show the poor performance of the antiquated district police force. I learnt later that this officer had a wife of German extraction. And on the declaration of hostilities in 1939, she was placed on the suspects' list and had to report her movements to the local police ! The police headquarters at Cuttack had made separate arrangements for her surveillance and in this matter the husband had not been taken into confidence. The District Superintendent, a full member of the local ruling junta, was not taken into confidence in various other important matters as well. He had therefore developed a kind of complex and would sneer at all attempts at improvements ! I was unaware of these details then and his attitude troubled me greatly. It was crystal clear that innovations and reforms were not in favour and merely a strong hand was required with which the political malcontents should be dealt with and kept in their proper places.

The police set-up in Orissa was very economical. At the head was the I.G. Police who was a glorified D.I.G., getting the salary which was slightly above that of the officers of the latter rank. He had the assistance of only two Superintendents of Police at his headquarters who looked after the entire C.I.D. and staff work, including control of the provincial armed police. The normal set-up in a province was many times more than this. As the number of districts in the province was only six, there was little problem of inspection for the I.G. and the S.Ps enjoyed the powers of a D.I.G., as there was no officer of that rank in the province. There were only two sub-divisional police officers, Rayaghada being the more important of the two. The sub-divisional police officer here had an importance somewhat like that of the S.P of a district in other provinces. This was a plus point for me.

The conflict between the money-lenders and the poor tribals was an ancient one. Not long ago there was a severe conflagration in the neighbouring districts of Ganjam, where men of the Sawra tribe were at loggerheads with the Pans, the money-lending business fraternity which had been exploiting them for long. The murder of one such Bania at the hands of a Paharia tribal in a remote corner of the sub-division therefore resulted in considerable furore at the district headquarters and seemed to have caused anxiety even to the Governor, who was the supremo. The incident caused a stir in the provincial vernacular press, there being no English daily in the entire province of Orissa. I motored part of the way, had an elephant ride, and later walked a good fifteen miles to reach the spot of the incident, only to find that it was a local quarrel and had no overtones of the conflict regarding which apprehensions were expressed in the press and in the senior administrative echelons. To complete my job, I had to tackle the tribals through three interpreters working in a series, the first translation being effected from the tribal language into Telugu, the second into Oriya, and finally the third in English. Hindi or Hindustani was hardly understood here. Even with my expertise in the Oriya language, I found that it was impossible for me to get the meaning of the words used without the assistance of the Oriya-English interpreter. My report was passed on to the highest administrative levels and even though interested groups would put a different interpretation on the happenings, the line taken by me was accepted and formed the basis of all government decisions. This was a great morale booster for me and showed the great reliance placed on the officers of the I.P. even though they might be junior in age and experience. A separate enquiry was later ordered at the level of special Assistant Agent in which the officer of the adjoining area cooperated in a big way. This concerned itself with revenue matters, and I was happy to find the unity of purpose of the senior civil service but the police lacked the esprit de corps, which should have been its hallmark. The cooperation that I got from my counterpart in the neighbouring area was extremely poor, but the two sub-divisional officers went hand in hand.

Going to the spot of the Paharia-Bania dispute, I had to pass via the backward Parwatipuram and Srikakulam (Chicacola) areas of the adjoining district of Vishakhapatnam. The State of Andhra Pradesh had not yet been carved out : it had not even been thought of. I could see in this area the rumbles of discontent and nascent revolt, which came prominently to notice about two decades later, under the leaders of the Naxalite movement. It aimed at demolishing the edifice of the administration supporting usurious moneylenders. At this stage my contact with the police in Madras presidency was highly illuminating. The police appeared to be a much more dreaded force in this area, and possibly more effective. It was customary here for heavy vehicles to stop aside when they espied a car coming from the opposite direction. Generally these cars would belong to one of the official fraternity possibly the police and due respect had to be shown to them ! I also learnt that the police in this area raised funds from all subordinate ranks with which they could look after the senior officials visiting the area while on official tours ! Conventional crimes appeared to be well under control compared to other parts of the country. On a visit to Vishakhapatnam later, I stayed at the rest-house of the Jeypore Samasthanam. I happened to leave a valuable ring in my room but found it intact after hours of absence. It could have been easily whisked away without any risk of detection, but criminals, would not dare lay their hands on property left in "official" guest houses. This was not so in Bihar, where even the Inspector General's residence was victimized on more than one occasion.

Jeypore estate which, covered the entire district of Koraput was the property of the Maharaja, who had this appellation as a hereditary title. This munificent Maharaja had contributed large sums of money towards the establishment of the Andhra University, of which he was ex-officio pro-chancellor for life. Mismanagement of the estate affairs had impoverished him greatly, and this was reflected in the maintenance of his palace. However, basically the Maharaja believed in simple living, more in keeping with the standards of his people. The Samasthanam, maintained a lavish guest house, which was provided with all the modern amenities. This was for the honoured guests only. Large areas of the forests in the estate were leased out to foreign firms and their executives were included in the V.I.P. list. While on a visit and staying in the guest-house, I was struck by the shabby behaviour of the manager of this firm—an Englishman. This dandified clerk was throwing his weight about and expressing disapproval of the eggs produced for his breakfast for no apparent reason, and he declared that he had the right to do so as the Maharaja was in debt to his firm. The General Manager of the estate was all the time making compromises with people such as this. The Dewan as he was designated, had a special knack of getting round people particularly foreigners. He played host to the numerous senior officers who visited Jeypore and ministered to their daily requirements. The servile behaviour of this functionary was not to my liking and yet it appeared that perhaps there was no way out for people such as he in their relations with the British officials and also the representatives of big business who were drawn mainly from England, and who went hand in hand with the officials. It appeared that I had to fit myself into this system. How I wished the Dewan and his subordinates, could be just friendly rather than servile! I found that another officer of my cadre, who was posted in the district behaved exactly like the Dewan towards his British superiors. He succeeded in becoming their favourite, obtained special treatment, and made good progress in the departmental hierarchy. I knew that such Indian officers would also look for servile behaviour from their juniors as they went up in seniority. This attitude would sound the death knell for any improvement even if power came our way.

The whimsical functioning of the administration stands out in my mind in an incident in which a Sub-Inspector of police was involved. The bus in which the S.I. and his family were travelling was detained at the local police station, causing serious inconvenience to the travelling public. During the war years i.e. from 1939 till 1945, government orders were that no police functionary should leave his post of duty unless he had been properly relieved of the same. This Sub-Inspector had a family problem and yet was not allowed to move away. He indicated the urgency of his problem and left by the bus but the vehicle was stopped near the police headquarter by the Superintendent of Police and the Sub-Inspector was pulled out unceremoniously. Not only was the police officer manhandled but his family was subjected to indignities. Not satisfied with this the Sub-Inspector was later prosecuted in a court of law for desertion. He was convicted by the local courts but got an acquittal from the High Court. The mental anguish through which he would have passed could well be imagined. This officer did not receive the sympathy of other police officers of his rank, leave aside his seniors. In the meanwhile the S.P. got all the kudos for firm handling of his officers. It was also clear that the judicial officers drawn from executive ranks were merely playing up to the senior administrative officers in the district, which meant the District Police Superintendent.

Interesting breaks in the drab day to day administrative work were provided by the visits of the Governor. On the Governor's visit to the district headquarters, when I was posted there as the S.P.'s aide after my posting at Rayaghada, the estate authorities arranged a bird-shoot. Following this was a lavish lunch and other entertainments. The senior officers were placed in a line, while the birds were driven from one end so that the shooters could take aim and bring them down. Not far from me was the heir apparent of the estate. To my surprise I found that he was shaking with fright as the birds were flying past. I realised later that a panther had been disturbed along with the birds and had sped past the Kumar Sahib. The Kumar Sahib's trepidation was that the panther might strike at the shooting party causing injuries and in the process he would lose all chance of getting titles etc. Action against the estate would also have ensued encumbered as it always was with debts and other liabilities. The Persian saying "Arrange for shooting a tiger, even if you are out for a jackal"—was fully exemplified in this episode. The Kumar Sahib breathed freely only after the panther had sped away in another direction without paying attention to the noise that was going on. Shikars as entertainment were often arranged by the richer sections of the community to curry favour with officials, who had the power to make or mar them. These were expensive but no official displeasure was attracted to such goings on as it was considered proper that the senior functionaries of the State should be looked after and entertained properly by the richer section of the community. Indeed a grand way of keeping the glory of the Raj in India which was rightly designated as the brightest jewel in the British Crown. But these frivolities were on their last legs what with popular discontent and even the aristocrats were feeling humiliated by the manner in which all this bandobast was asked for and accepted with condescension by the ruling elite.

Talking about tigers, on one occasion when I was still at Rayaghada the mail did not arrive from the district headquarters for two days. I was due to make a visit to that place the next day and leaving my office in the afternoon, I had proposed to drive through the cool hours of the day so as to reach the destination before dinner time. As it got dark I espied two bright lights some distance away on the road running along the ghat. I then realised that it was a full grown tiger sprawled across the drive way. I sounded the horn more than once, it was with great difficulty that the intruder could be persuaded to let me go. On going across to the next village, I found the dak runner lazing away. He reported that the tiger was prowling near the road for the whole day and therefore he could not go across to the next village to hand over mail to his successor in the line. Such intrusions were not infrequent in this area. The beat and habits of most tigers were known and life was adjusted accordingly by the locals unless the beast took to mauling human beings or attacking human habitations for prey. The daily reports prepared by the police stations indicated the position regarding the behaviour of the feline species as well. It had comments about the weather, the state of the crops, and other allied matters. On another trip through this area, I was stopped by some simple looking tribals who exhibited two cubs—*bagh pilla*—which they wanted me to take over. I did not have the time or inclination to take this on but I was told that near Cuttack, an old landlord had collected quite a menagerie of the wild life in his palace. The revenue authorities could not visit his palace to collect arrears of taxes for fear the animals might attack them. This Zamindar later on passed his possessions to the zoos in India after a good deal of persuasion. He died, heirless unwept, unlamented, and unsung.

The British administrative system in the country was also run on the model of the army like the I.P. working on the model of army commissions. Therefore considerable attention was paid to the armed component of the police force. Even the civil police cadres were so fashioned that they could be converted into armed units almost immediately. There was provision in the district police formation, of what was known as the mobilised contingent. This consisted of a drill of withdrawing approximately twenty five per cent of the personnel from each post and arming them forthwith. Their unit formation was based on a pre-arranged plan and they were given periodical refresher courses. A considerable amount of importance was necessarily given to the commanders of this armed force. At the district level the Superintendent of Police functioned as the Supreme Commander. The District Collector was busy with other affairs of administration and the job of law keeping had necessarily to be left entirely to the care of the district S.P. Although on paper subordinated to the district officer, the Superintendent of Police had to function as the local director of affairs. He was also the conscience-keeper of the district officer. Government communications were sent out to the D.M., but nothing of any importance could happen unless the S.P. was in the counsel. The Superintendent of Police was thus a much dreaded (and respected) authority at the district level, and a cut above all the other district level officers. His word was law, and functionaries like the District Medical Officer or the Engineer had to be specially careful in their deportment towards him. Any lapse and the latter could put them in serious trouble. As all matters of moment had to be investigated by the Superintendent of Police, the other officers were fully aware of the power of his pen. His reports could be damaging to any one in the district and this included the Collector. These reports could be entirely subjective, but it must be stated that such a contingency rarely arose. The reports were so highly trustworthy that these were in effect the last word in the administrative process. At superior levels, only a mere counter-signature was needed—a *dhobi* mark. I had noticed this even as a junior field officer, in regard to my report on the trouble in the tribal areas. It was also not unusual for very senior district officers to go to junior Police Superintendents of their district to take their advice on almost all matters before sending reports to Government.

I found in my case that a very senior district officer, F.E.A. Taylor (of the Indian Civil Service) would not send any report or even an important letter to the provincial government without bringing me into the picture and having my full concurrence—this when I was merely officiating as S.P., being substantively only a sub-divisional police officer and a junior one at that. It was the administrative philosophy that such should be the case, or else the fabric of general administration could not have gone on so smoothly so far. The system broke down soon after independence, though the administrative format continued as of yore. This is greatly responsible at present for the malaise in governmental work.

The formation of district armed units in vogue then was completely different from what prevails now. The armed force consisted of sections generally of the strength of one head constable, and eight to ten constables. There were about five to six sections sanctioned for each district. Where the demand for armed guards was higher, an additional strength of three or four more sections was added. The number of constables in each section provided for about two being absent on leave. Thus each section would always have about seven constables available under one head constable. Four sections formed the charge of a Jamadar, who was equated with a junior commissioned officer of the Army and carried the same badges of rank. The entire unit in each district was placed under a retired British Army officer of the rank of sergeant, and he was designated as a Sergeant Major or a Reserve Inspector. He acted much as a Captain would function vis-a-vis a platoon. This armed force was given re-bored army rifles. These were converted into smooth-bore muskets of .410 bore. The muskets had to have special ammunition which was manufactured in the Army Ordnance factory. The most interesting type of ammunition was the buckshot, which carried a large number of small pellets. The result, though injuries may be caused to those hit, death was generally not possible unless a shot hit some very vital organ. Being a smooth bore weapon, the shots could not carry far and a hundred yards was the outside range of the weapon. This type of fire-arms worked admirably for keeping the civilians under control without causing large scale loss of life. It even permitted the mob being allowed to come near enough as instructions for dispersal could not be relayed over a long distance. Belhailers and things of that variety were unknown then. The bugle was the best that could be used to attract attention and the gramophone type amplifier could be used to broadcast orders of the authorities. The force performed its drill in fours. Only after World War II was well on the way that drill in threes was introduced on the army pattern, in the police as well. This new drill was formulated keeping in view the combat groups in the army i.e. the pincer group and the sections on the two sides to protect the flanks. Such movements were hardly relevant to the police but no expertise on problems particular to the police had been developed and therefore in the matter of drill etc. the army pattern had to be aped. The only exception was with regard to tear-smoke units which had just been introduced experimentally for dealing with violent mobs. However, each province had its own additional special reserves, which were formed entirely on the army pattern. Four sections formed a platoon, three platoons formed a company, and about five companies formed a battalion. Those reserves, contrary to the weaponry carried by district reserves, were equipped with army pattern .303 rifles and even a couple or so of light machine guns were provided, more as show-pieces than for actual use. Some grenade firing rifles were given on the lines of the equipment of a light infantry unit of the Army.

The organisation of the district armed police and also of the state reserves was not satisfactory and the drill in fours appeared to be more in the nature of a pantomime. Its substitute, the drill in threes was more mystifying although it did simplify the words of command and the various drill movements on the parade ground, items in which I had been fully trained at the training institution. I would like to make reference to an interesting form of movement on the parade ground, which was known as extended-order drill. It consisted in extending a section over a long stretch of parade ground and in moving them forward in single file or in one line by whistle signals or by raising the arms. Except causing inconvenience to armed constables, who were required to perform this parade, the entire exercise appeared to be completely futile. I have not known of a single occasion in which these funny drill movements could be brought to use. I would like to mention another interesting drill, known as riot-drill. This consisted of sending out an advance party to warn the mob against illegal intent, and this was followed by the armed forces moving forward and forming in two ranks, ready to fire. The subsequent drill included picking up of the injured etc. There could not be a more unimaginative method of dealing with crowds and I had the mortification of seeing during my training that a procession, bent on violating the route laid down for it, started to grapple with the armed constables even before any warning could be administered, not to speak of the unit getting ready for the firing order etc. The mob melted away after a few lathi blows were hurled at them. Apparently futile methods of training were employed and the armed police force revelled in it. The idea was merely to train to obey orders and not to present likely situations. With 1942 came a large number of raids on police posts, which could not be repelled by the unpractical training given to the constables. Now police posts were protected much on the lines of the army posts. Sand bagging and trench digging became the order of the day. Armed police guards, particularly those in treasuries and important offices and residences of VIPs which included the District Superintendent, were taught the new procedures of check, in which no risk was taken, and all persons visiting the guard area were subjected to severe personal checks. The danger, however, was always there of the armed men themselves turning against the persons whom they were expected to protect like what happened in 1857. The need of the hour was the devising of simple drills for constables to make them obey orders and competent to perform jobs like surrounding and combing villages or searching houses. In any case their morale required to be built up first. At the higher policy making levels, these items did not attract much attention. This showed the direction in which the wind was blowing, a realisation that the Raj would not last long. It was considered that the confusing training should continue so that a breakdown in the management of affairs under the new dispensation, would be more likely.

An interesting feature of police work in the tribal belt, where the police force had not penetrated far enough, is worth mentioning. In these areas the tribal courts continued to function and small matters did not bother the general administration. However, an armed contingent of policemen numbering about thirty to forty, which was a big force by the standards then prevailing, were shown round the tribal belt in a foot-march for about a week or so. This was known as "showing the flag". It was intended to impress on the tribal population the need for remaining within the bounds of law. Knowing the capacity of these poor tribals to cause trouble, this show of flag appeared to be flamboyant nonsense. However, the experience gave the policeman a taste of quasi-military life under canvas. I recollect that on the first march of this kind in the district (Koraput) where I was posted, I succeeded in bagging the first panther of my career. We could also get a python and its skin was used for the District Band. The march led us through interesting hilly and forest countryside which according to one of the officers going with us, had been the route of the epic hero Rama's journey after his banishment from Ayodhya. There were other interesting facets : the personal servant (bearer) of one of the officers would pompously put on his livery including turban when on the move and promptly discard these on reaching the destination. He would appear in a vest and short dhoti for serving his master. This interesting bearer sported the initials of his boss in Roman character upside down and caused not a little mirth amongst the senior members and the force. He carried a "W" in place of the "M", he should have had.

I was moved to the district headquarters now. The daily routine of a junior field officer in the district office was rather drab. There was the usual morning parade following by attendance in office, with a break for lunch. The evening hours were employed in playing games with the men, hockey or football. Sometimes checking up on the families in the lines was required. While on the round, the members of the families stood in silence watching the Indian Saheb, who was no different from the British master as he could not even speak their lingo. Sometimes there was a game of tennis in the local club with the top brass. It was customary to let the senior officers lead to keep them in good humour. In the bigger centres, there would be a round of bridge at the Gymkhana Club. It did not appear that a war was on in which we were involved. However, the realities of the war were brought home in 1942, following the bombing along the coastal area of the province on a convoy carrying supplies from Calcutta to Madras. This bombardment caused serious unquiet in the State capital and I was posted there to meet the emergent situation. On arrival I found that Cuttack had been declared a non-family station. The senior British officers had already sent their families to the distant hills and the Indian families were sent away to relations staying in areas away from the coastal belt. The flat spin in which the administration went showed that victory or defeat, the administration in the country was on its last legs. The traditional efficiency of the administration had gone. About this time, there was a false alarm of a landing by the Japanese along the coast in the district of Balasore. The result was that the District Magistrate and the Superintendent of Police promptly scuttled their records and currency notes available in the treasury and rushed to areas at least a hundred miles away from the coast. This was fantastic, but I was happy to find that no questions were asked about the bona fides of these officers. The currency notes could have been whisked away by any of the functionaries, which could be the case in the new dispensation that was to follow, but even a suspicion of such eventuality did not arise. During these troubled days, albeit short, the foreign group continued to get together and in this even the Sergeant Major had a place. The Indian element collected together in their own rendezvous. It irked me that this was confined to the very senior officers, but even a subordinate of the status of Sergeant Major was given such consideration by the ruling group. He was much pampered : he was provided with excellent living accommodation but I was left to fend for myself as I was on special duty and could not be allotted an official residence. As a supernumerary in the higher levels of administration, I found that my function was somewhat like that of an army reservist. There was nothing special for me to do except to watch. Socially there was a vacuum, culturally there was no activity and professionally it was a complete sinecure. I attended office to glean the rumours that were afloat, and transacted little business. Traditionally senior officers were not to take office work too seriously as routine work went on more or less like clock-work. Unfortunately in the succeeding dispensation, the same lethargy in taking decisions at superior levels continued. Decision-making at this time was a simple affair and was controlled at the apex. This would be unsuitable for a democracy and I was wondering what would happen. As it was the old system was allowed to go on in the new situation !

On the bombardment of the convoy, I literally took leave of Cuttack for about ten days and moved from one police station to another along the coast-line to take stock of what had been salvaged. There was anxiety on the part of the local population to grab whatever came their way, including buoys, and pieces of furniture. There was no scare amongst the rural poor. Back in town, I learnt how the Indian District Magistrate was told off by the Chief Secretary for his inability to get along the coastline while a junior policeman had done it. His visits to the hospital to see the injured navy personnel were not approved of as this work was in the domain of secretariat personnel. Then a Defence-department liaison officer was posted at Cuttack, an officer of the rank of Wing Commander; he was the Chief Controller and advised the Governor. The power that he wielded in swaying action at the provincial headquarters, gave this officer the appellation of "Wind Commander."

A very striking feature at this time was the acute inferiority complex of Indian officers. However, unlike the British element, the Indians always worked at cross purposes. This pained me greatly. As noted earlier the Indian officers of the I.C.S. and the I.P., posted at Cuttack had made a habit of getting together in the evenings. Being a non-family station the ladies had left the station but the wife of the District Magistrate stuck on. One evening, she was told by another member of this conclave that her husband would also become a grass-widower now as the non-family rules were being applied strictly. This not too young lady was in great temper on this comment as she did not like the mention of the word widower in relation to her husband.

Followed the Quit India movement of 1942—the activity in Orissa consisted mainly of attempts at cutting down trees in the Reserves. I was moved to Ganjam district to tackle this problem and also lend a hand to local officers as the situation in the provincial capital had improved considerably. No incursion of any sort materialised from the Japanese as anticipated. The coastline in Ganjam presented a picture of avid preparation with the setting up of dummy anti-aircraft guns all along. The police posted along the coastline reported to have sighted flickering lights somewhat away from the shoreline one night. On the succeeding day, patrolling the coastal area, a senior police officer espied some Mongoloid looking persons moving suspiciously. On being interrogated they promptly immolated themselves by taking potassium cyanide, which they carried on their person. There was a large haul of counterfeit Indian currency notes from these agents. Apparently the intention was to pass it on to local links. This incident promptly resulted in the visit to the area of the Inspector General. In regard to this area special helio-signal equipment and signal lamps had been provided earlier. It was an education to see the Inspector General moving along these posts, enthusing the local officers and all this on cycle and on foot. This was indicative of the superior ranks setting an example and getting down to the job without employing motor vehicles, which were easily available. Thus the I.G. got near the working groups and set an example of hard work. Within a few years' time, the post-independence period was to show how callously and carelessly government vehicles and equipment were used for personal work by senior police functionaries and even by juniors. There was a mad race to use government property as if it were personal property. About this time, the detenus in the Central Jail at Berhampur, mainly those who had participated in the forest felling operations, resorted to an agitation inside the jail. They were led by Bishwanath Das, later to become the Chief Minister of the State and also Rajyapal in U.P. Their grievances did not cover fresh ground and were confined mainly to the insufficient rations and poor accommodation. Yet much was made of it and even a jail-break was attempted. I visited the area with a small body of armed police and this force had to be lined up ready to shoot if the prisoners persisted in their efforts to break through the jail gate. Bishwanath Das had been earlier placed under arrest by me. I had the impression that he was a soft spoken satyagrahi, and a true Gandhian who was opposed to the tactics of violence. Mahatma Gandhi had not foreseen violent action following the Quit-India call. The violence in the jail therefore surprised me. It was entirely the result of Bishwanath Das's persuasion that this agitation at the jail-gate came to a halt. The prisoners were thereafter placed in special enclosures so that trouble of this nature could not recur. I found the jail staff entirely submissive to the police and prepared to act according to their behests. The Jail Superintendent had no hesitation in calling for the guidance of the District Police Superintendent as he knew that this had the support of the District Magistrate and the approval of the government as well. Bishwanath Das recollected all this years later when I met him at a district conference of Rotary International that he addressed. About this time, the coastal belt was visited by the Viceroy, Lord Wavell. Palpably as a sequel to a severe cyclone which hit the coastline, the idea was to reconnoitre the area for defence preparedness. Large scale security arrangements had to be made for the Viceroy. Not knowing what questions may be asked, the District Superintendent also collected statistics of all varieties including that of the number of trees which were uprooted, the number of crimes committed during the period etc. Security arrangements for the special train were provided by the armed police, and a pilot engine was kept for extra protection on the track. Chowkidars and villagers lined the track throughout. The arrangements were foolproof but greatly demonstrative. I found for the first time detectives from the special branch garbed as members of the Viceroy's personal staff to keep watch. The Viceroy did not ask a single question of the Superintendent of Police but preparedness was the essence of things. I also realised that government consisted of fifty per cent effective work and the other fifty per cent was demonstration. This kept up the prestige of the Raj.

I now wanted to go on short leave, for personal reasons but things being not entirely normal. I was not permitted to go. However, orders of this nature had to issue with the approval of the Governor who was responsible for the welfare of the top services. As the refusal took place first and the file was sent to him later, the Governor administered a rebuff to the I.G. and all. Result : not only was my leave allowed as it was for urgent personal reasons, the Inspector General had to make an apologia, enquiring from me when I would like to go. I availed of the leave without the formality of a notification, which was generally necessary. My experience later, nearly two decades after the attainment of independence was entirely different. Leave was officially and properly granted to me for going abroad in 1961. I was then a D.I.G. Police. For no obvious reason, except perhaps the whims of the Chief Minister, I was told, when my preparations were completed, that I should not go as some Muslim festival would be on during the period. The leave could be obtained only on the recommendation of another senior Minister in the State. This was done though no apprehension existed justifying the leave of a senior D.I.G. to be held up. The State Governor was not in the picture in this case. But when President's rule was introduced later with the Rajyapal as the kingpin of the administration, this dignitary rather than keep the interest of the service, conspired with the politicians to upset the posting of senior police officers. There appeared to be a complete somersault in administrative ethos in such matters.

During his annual camp in the sub-division, the Governor made a visit to the farm of a landlord, who was highly educated and held the degrees of M.A. and B.L. to his credit. He was a Dewan Bahadur to boot. Having shown the Governor round the farm and its ancillaries -- this was in many ways a model farm—and while bidding adieu the Dewan Bahadur expressed his gratitude by saying that he was honoured by the visit of the Governor and his "Governess" ! The lady kept her temper but it was not difficult to discern the change in her demeanour. This was specially so as we learnt that her ladyship had during her younger years been a governess in England. There was another incident at a dinner party hosted by the Governor. A comparatively lesser educated, but senior forest officer thanked the Governor at the end of the function by saying that he had a good time with the Governor's wife, whom he designated as "Madam Governess"! Later this officer received a severe reprimand from his department. His name was permanently removed from the list of invitees to Government House functions. This officer appeared at the dinner party in a borrowed achkan sporting a pair of trousers of dissimilar hue. There were critical comments on this even from Indian officers, who frowned at any sartorial liberties at formal functions.

The local landlord fraternity vied with each other in entertaining the Governor when on his official visits. Being invited to a party at the Governor's camp was a great honour, to be celebrated even late at the residence after the function ended. Not content with what had been imbibed there, of which the quantity naturally had to be reasonable, they usually started on a drinking spree on their return home. On this occasion people of the neighbourhood were roused at night by loud reports of gun-shooting. It transpired that the entire furore was over these satraps competing with each other with their shooting pieces to see whose shot went higher up in the air! One of the notable members of this fraternity, displayed a chart of protocol at the entrance of his palace grounds indicating the distance which he would come out to, to greet the intending visitors. This naturally depended greatly on their rank and status. A driving ramp to the first floor of the house was set up by this individual so that he could alight from the car straight into his gorgeous bedroom on that floor.

An interesting system of the village community assisting the law and order forces was in vogue in the hilly areas bordering the coastal strip in the district of Ganjam. Each village would send a young man to the local police station for a period of a week, having his tour of duty for the entire day for three days and on an equal number of nights. These volunteers performed patrols in the police station area as required by the Station House Officer, known locally as officer-in-charge. The number of such volunteers was quite considerable for each police station and therefore it was not necessary to employ whole time stipendiary staff for this work. The interesting provision was that if the villages failed to send their representative, known as the paik, they would pay compensation which formed a sizable fund at each police station for utilising in crime prevention work, including providing some basic items of identification for the paiks on duty. These patrolmen brought local intelligence about their area, which was invaluable and resulted in the crime rate being reasonably low and the criminals being quickly brought to book. The system was indicative of the citizen's responsibility for grassroots police work and his involvement with the paid staff. They could even be called on to patrol in areas away from their village though within the same police stations. This implied a modicum of corporate responsibility. The police officers were assured of local support as the village paik was nominated and selected by the Panchayat of the village. However, I found that the system was being given up and replaced by policemen, fully paid and uniformed, as far as possible. This was a sphere in which some experimentation was called for.

5

THE ROVING COMMANDER

THE POSITION as District Superintendent of Police was obtained by an officer of the Indian Police then, much in the nature of the assignment of a relieving station master on the Indian railways. With the large number of railway stations and the possibility of casualties of various sorts, the railway management, largely under the aegis of the State, had to be carried on by keeping a band of prospective station masters in each railway system who for about two to three years in their career went about on a relieving job, till they could be firmly settled at one station for a normal tenure. The number of district charges in the police in any state cadre, and the requirement of long leave specially during the hot weather for a large foreign component of this service, required that a senior Assistant Superintendent of Police should be on a roving job like that of the station master for about a year or so. Literally the officer concerned had to live out of suitcases, as in each station furnished accommodation was available—the furniture belonging to the predecessor who expected to come back to the same station after his leave. This procedure also enabled the juniors to obtain experience in holding charge of a district Superintendent's office, for which no detailed training was given. The system was based on the thesis of seniority and "into the shoes" procedure. The Superintendent of Police was a rank of superior command, requiring initiative, but the giving of general directions to the subordinate formations was a matter of great responsibility and required adequate experience in practical work. No genius was needed.

There was thus no question of weeding out unfit elements at this stage and the switch over to the superior job was automatic.

The Superintendent of Police had a prominent position in the administrative set up of the district. All visiting personages had necessarily to contact him on coming to the area. His word was law for his subordinates, and he acted more like an army commander. His intimate contact with the CID, was an indication of his chores of crime prevention, and influence over political goings on, the CID (special branch) being the agency for collection of political intelligence.

My first officiating charge as District S.P. was in 1943 in the very district in which I had worked about a year back as an Assistant S.P. in the sub-division and at the headquarters of that district as well. I was welcomed with open arms by the minions of Jeypore Samasthanam. The Dewan of the estate was the first to come along and break the news that I was the first Indian Superintendent of the District. I was requested always to avail of the guest houses of the estate, during my tours, a procedure which, I was mollified to find, had government approval. This was not a case of corruption but of merely keeping up the prestige of the administration. My predecessor was the same S.P., who had a German wife and who was not exactly a persona grata with the ruling clan. My posting was therefore a relief to all concerned. The subordinates had had to put up with his whimsical ways, and they felt mighty happy now.

When I got into the details of work (after taking over), I was surprised to find references being made about top leaders of the Congress and in particular Jawahar Lal Nehru in highly derogatory terms. Pt. Nehru's western upbringing and British contacts notwithstanding, he was commonly branded as unreliable and a Communist fellow-traveller. When I explained that in him was the only hope of the British elements in India as Jawaharlal had a soft corner for things British, the country where he had his early education, nobody was convinced. 'My predecessor was a suspect and in the twilight of the Raj an Indian officer, had a special position as he was expected to know things about the leaders of the Congress which could help stem the impending disaster. Yet in this matter, my opinion did not cut much ice. Quite a large number of European officers were already taking furlough to get away to East Africa or other colonies, where they could go on much as they were doing in India. They were all praise for only those Indian members of the service who were devoted to the British Raj. Some of the Indian incumbents had even anglicised the names of their children : Prem being called Pram and Preeti as Pretty. One such officer, of the Engineering Service—a Eurasian—was processing his case for shifting to Australia by establishing that he was 51 per cent White. The White Australia policy kept away the browns and the blacks from that continent.

It was somewhat of a frustrating experience to have to formulate schemes for the protection of foreign elements in the district in case of a mass uprising. In this scheme even subordinates of foreign extraction had an important place. Senior Indian officers like myself were included, but that appeared to be somewhat of an eye-wash. This scheme, an important secret document, made provision for every little detail based on the experience of the siege of the Residency in Lucknow in 1857. The conservatism of the British and their faith in planning was patent.

At this time, I made a journey from Koraput to Cuttack to attend an important meeting. Getting into the Madras Mail at Vizianagram railway station in a first class compartment, I realised that the other lone occupant of a berth in that compartment was Chakravarti Rajagopalachari. Being one of the dissidents, he had not been taken into custody with the other Congress leaders. He was in fact proceeding to Cuttack to deliver a course of lectures at the Ravenshaw College there. As I was in uniform, I felt that it may be misconstrued that ultimately C.R. had also been nabbed and was being escorted to some prison outside the Madras Presidency. Perhaps some violence may occur but I was spared this. At all stops of the train, C.R. would stand at the entrance of the compartment and address his admirers who came along with floral offerings. C.R. was studying the Gita and while in conversation with him, I found the deep insight he had of the administrative machine. He was fully posted with the working of the I.P. cadre and expressed surprise that an all-India service should be required for the police. The unity of the country, he thought, would be achieved by cultural integration in which the Hindi language had a prominent part to play. He was a great protagonist of Hindi as the national language of the country. It was unfortunate that the language jingoists made C.R. change his views on this point later.

Even though it appeared that it would not take long for the devolution of power in Indian hands, the District S.P. was still expected to behave like the old *koihais* of the heyday of the British colonial regime. The armed wing of the police was the S.P's preserve and in its working the District Magistrate had no say. The Superintendent had to look to the welfare of the men: organising cooperative shops, work centres for the women, and schools for the children. Doing manual work at the residence of the Superintendent was considered an honour by policemen and not a '*begar*'—unpaid labour. Not that this was ever considered necessary as manual labour was indeed cheap and available for the mere asking. Even technically trained workmen, had a very low place in the payment schedule. There was a system in which the smartest constable on the morning parade was selected for day-orderly duty at the S.P's residence. There was a very stiff competition for this position and the job required to be done was merely to attend to the dignitary at his house, even to polishing his shoes and looking after his household furniture. In later years, perhaps due to its abuse by senior officers and the development of extra departmental channels for getting advancement, this system had to be given up. Even the orderly system has been assailed as undemocratic and not in accordance with the State policy of socialism.

The systematic working of the confidential section in the office of the Superintendent of Police was remarkable, and about this I had not had much training earlier. The general office was not a going concern though. The confidential work required a good deal of the time of the half educated British Superintendent. But to the Indian counterpart, having high educational standards, this was a mere bagatelle. As for the work in the field it was carried on like a generalist though one felt sure that specialisation was called for. I tried to imbibe knowledge from the literature that was then available, but this was scarce. No assistance was available from the provincial headquarters. To mention one item, there was no system of keeping records about criminals. The system in vogue was the product of the genius of half baked, British seniors, who had neither the training nor the educational background to support them. This was a field of work which attracted me straightway but all this was somewhat premature in the existing clime. The knowledge of the English language of the British

N.C.O. inducted in the police, was extremely inadequate ; and this worried me to some extent. I had the temerity to point this out to one of my subordinates. I was told off by the I.G. that this was hardly necessary. Instead of any reprimand this ex-army H.C.O. got a pat on his back from the boss, which in many ways was a slap on my face. There was no use protesting as the I.G. had the last word in the department. Indeed this was the sheet-anchor of the discipline in the force. This system has gone to pieces now. Also the S.P. as yet was the most reliable instrument of government. The report was the last word, but the experience in the country after independence is different ; these reports were thrown aside for personal reasons. The reports of third grade politicians were read with great respect, instead. The S.P. has gone down therefore in the level of integrity and incorruptibility as well.

It was the refrain of British I.C.S. and I.P. officers who worked with me, that they had waited in vain for a bribe to be offered to them, even though it was well understood that corruption was rampant in the subordinate Indian cadres. Even the British N.C.O. working in the armed police appeared to be incorruptible in more ways than one. The police constable worked for him at his bungalow but that was about all. This N.C.O. made purchases for his department in a big way but I do not know of any case in which he made money in this process: something not nncommon in India now.

The period of service as roving Superintendent brought me into picture of the deteriorating Hindu-Muslim relations. I was posted as Superintendent in a district in north Bihar during the pre-independence period, after my deputation to Orissa. A serious Hindu-Muslim conflagration developed in this district on the occasion of Ramnavmi—a Hindu festival. The Muslim crowd ran amuck throwing brickbats and refuse on the image of the deity. Almost the entire armed police at the district headquarters had to be rushed to the area of conflagration which was located on the border of Purnea district. The Commandant of an armed police unit was hurriedly sent there from the provincial headquarters with a large force to collate armed police work. The District Magistrate and the S.P. from neighbouring Purnea also made a visit ostensibly to help but the British Superintendent confined himself to making derogatory remarks about the incompetent Indian magistrate of his district, whom he chose to ignore. He had no hesitation in confronting the Indian District Magistrate of my area as well. The British Commandant of armed police and this British Superintendent of Police both had some secret consultations which indicated that they were interested more in the conflagration being intensified in certain areas rather than in bringing it under control. They would support the Muslim elements even though they appeared to be initially in the wrong box. I was lucky, however, in bringing the situation quickly under control with my limited resources and then requested the newly inducted elements to promptly withdraw. The British officers would even sow seeds of indiscipline among the junior Indian officers, encouraging them to confront their seniors if they did not belong to their own religious community. These officers were greatly frustrated in their attempt in this direction. Later on Muslim army units were inducted in the area to ensure even-handed justice to the Muslim community, which was indicated as the oppressed group although it was they who had taken the lead in creating the disturbances. It was lucky that I could manage to shake off the army units too. These disturbances showed that the official policy was to lead the events into a channel where internecine warfare may develop between the two major religious communities in the country. This was in a way to reverse the process of cultural fusion of the two communities, that had taken great strides towards progress. "Divide and rule"—this was epitomised in a big way.

Going to the spot of the trouble with the armed police force, the D.M. and I could see some rioters only about a hundred yards away, a few miles off from the scene of the trouble. The armed party promptly took position and fired but they were unlucky to miss the gang leader, who was riding away on a pony. He was identified as a local bigwig and he avoided arrest for some time. He was a close relation of a senior I.C.S. officer in the state, which he considered gave him a certain amount of immunity from the law. He was disillusioned, as he admitted, when he was caught. His relation would not help him by making *pairvi* in his favour. However, the position was to change very soon after attainment of independence when *pairvi* became the accepted mode of work and in fact the grease of the wheels of administration. Sans *pairvi* there was to be no chance of even getting your due, howsoever good the case might be.

There was a clear indication in 1946, when all this happened that not much time would elapse before the reins of administration would come into Indian hands. But it was astounding to find how political leaders, who were placed temporarily at the helm of affairs in the province, started quickly promoting elements of their own caste to important posts. The newly promoted officers had hardly any understanding of the problems with which they were faced. They indulged in petty politicking much to the detriment of the morale and discipline of the police. Members of the provincial service, now promoted to posts which were normally filled by officers of the Indian Civil Service, and Indian Police, started a wrangle about their taking over charge in the districts. The residence of the provincial Chief Minister—in the interim government he was designated as Prime Minister, was a veritable *mela* with his cronies trotting round the place distributing favours on behalf of the boss. They could arrange meetings of officers with the chief to press their personal cases. This was readily allowed and promotions and transfers were arranged on the spot, the orders being issued on yellow printed sheets known as buff-sheets to the Appointments Department for issuance of the notifications in the Provincial Gazette.

Connected with the prevailing situation on the eve of independence in August 1947 was the disarray in the district administration. In my district, a new District Magistrate was posted by wire-pulling at the provincial headquarters. The new incumbent would not be left behind in the garnering of the root. He came along with a copy of the order to assume his magisterial duties. But the old incumbent would not vacate office as he wanted a copy of the usual orders from head office and also to know the place of his new posting. There was no trace of such an order. These two senior members of the provincial service, now in the "listed" cadre, considered that I, a chip of the old block though young in years, should be able to settle their dispute. I advised telephonic contact with the Chief Secretary but he could be of no help either as the connected order was still in transit between the Chief Minister's Office and the Secretariat. The new incumbent had to mark time for well nigh a fortnight before formal orders came, also indicating the posting of the older incumbent. It was a sad sight to see subordinates moving between two founts of authority at the district headquarters, engaged in conspiracies of various sorts not knowing which way the matters would settle. Once they learnt of the despatch of the orders from Patna in favour of the new incumbent who was marking time, the older officer got cold shouldered all round and could come to me alone for solace. He thought that I was not afflicted by any partisan considerations. Altogether the situation appeared to me to be jocular and a pointer to the shape of things to come. It would be the old tune of the pre-British era when government functionaries were the figureheads of local cronies enjoying the support of the big ones. The service of the government had implied a considerable amount of *izzat* (dignity), and power, and authority, as also stability in tenure and functions. This was not to be now and service would possibly mean servitude, with the guiding light of local luminaries who, basking in the sunshine of the provincial leaders, might act in an entirely subjective way. My fears were well founded as later experience showed.

Saharsa, where I was posted, was the hide-out of the rebels during the 1942 Quit-India Movement. The terrain, the Kosi river belt, was difficult of access, and in fact this district was carved out to control matters with adequate competence. The dissident socialists of the Congress camp led by Jayaprakash Narayan (J.P.), had considerable hold here. J.P. came along to Saharsa and addressed a series of public meetings. One meeting was held near the railway inspection house, where I was living in the absence of any other accommodation. I could hear Jayaprakash Narayan's address from the verandah of the Inspection House. After the meeting was over, J.P. came to the Inspection House to wash before entraining for his journey out. He was accompanied by his associates, some of whom had been marked for violent activities—one carried a hockey stick in token of his creed. J.P. was given some throat pastilles and a glass of water before he set out. He warned me that his presence in this bungalow may be misconstrued by those in power. I could hardly think this possible and was greatly surprised to find that intelligence reports actually dubbed me as a sympathiser of socialists and to an extent a supporter of J.P. and what he stood for. Indeed it would have been highly discourteous on our part not to offer a glass of water to J.P. The Hindu philosophy of life which guides us lays down that a guest should be treated as an incarnation of God. J.P. was no rebel or insurgent but a leader of an important party which hadb een a part of the ruling group only a short while ago. His party had not been banned and I had not associated myself with him except to offer the rudimentary courtesy that should be given to a traveller. I felt nonplussed and could not comprehend how I should behave in a similar situation.

An interesting episode in this district was the inauguration of a hospital at its headquarters. This district headquarters was started from scratch and for several years there was no official building to boast of, much less a public hospital. When the institution was set up, there were no patients to cater for, as large areas around were completely uninhabited. The hospital in fact was set up to boost the chances of election from the areas of the local Congress leader. And the elections were round the corner with the likely grant of independence to the country. The inauguration was made with fanfare. The hospital had no beds, and some were borrowed from the local gentry and also from the small police hospital. The inaugurating dignitary was fully aware of the implications of the move and in this the new district officer was a conspirator. What a gross exhibition of window-dressing !

About this time another important event was the foundation laying of the construction work on the Kosi Barrage project. The Kosi was the river of sorrow of north Bihar, oscillating in a range of more than a hundred miles. This area became one sandy stretch, with channels of the river changing their course from year to year. The ceremony was performed by Dr. Rajendra Prasad, who was then a Minister in the Central Government. He travelled in a special carriage on the train from the Railway district headquarters at Samastipur, the scene of the murder of Railway Minister L.N. Mishra nearly three decades later. As the train wound its way to the base where the inauguration ceremony was to be convened, it appeared like a serpentine mass of humanity travelling in all possible places inside and outside the moving carriages. The helpless railway employees could do nothing in the matter. Again the shape of things to come ! On the occasion, the train carried the Prime Minister of Bihar and a large number of central ministers also. I was astounded to find that they considered there was nothing unusual or wrong in the way things were going on. In this belt relief had to be provided yearly to the flood-affected people. The chief problem was of reaching the daily rations to the people perched on trees. However, the people at the receiving end would refuse to accept the ration packets, if they did not contain "pan" and the brand of raw tobacco which was taken with it! The people were used to travelling free by train at their own risk and lived almost entirely on state subsidy. The railway system in the area was managed by a public limited concern with bases in England. In spite of free rides, they made adequate profit as running costs were low and the haulage of freight was colossal, considering the thick population in the belt. The line has since been taken on by the central government, and there is no change in the working system, but the profits have dwindled as the wages of the working staff have been raised and their number has proliferated. Perhaps this line would be in the red now. L.N. Mishra, a mere nobody then, later escalated into prominence and Saharsa has been converted into a divisional headquarters.

The district administration was in effect run by the local Congress who led both the judicial and executive wings of administration by the nose. It would be entirely at their peril if the subordinates went against the wishes of this group. Naturally corruption was the order of the day and not without the knowledge of the senior politicians. A back-bencher who ruled the roost in one of the sub-divisional towns, had assumed so much importance that he came to be designated unofficially as additional S.D.O. The S.D.O. combined in himself both executive and judicial functions. He played to the tune of this politician and in the process had a glorious time with splendid prospects of promotion. He made a tidy pile for himself too. This gentleman was well-connected and was from the northern sector of the district. He could count a large number of police-history-sheeters among his cohorts. A local sub-inspector of police went for one of them in his attempt to set matters straight in spite of the S.D.O.'s support to them. The result was a series of cases in which he was involved. Ultimately this poor subordinate retired from service in despair. The political set got on merrily and the politician, an uncle of Shri L.N. Mishra later became the state Congress president with all the influence that this position could carry. The younger elements, who prided on calling themselves socialists, provided the rift in the lute and came into open conflict with these leaders who had assumed positions of advantage. It was some time before they could come out in the open as the opposing group.

The junior members of the disciplined police force were aghast at the antics of their seniors who believed in making hay while the sun shines. My predecessor had left the district with a large packet of presents including cows and goats ! The constables were traditionally addressed as *tum* (singular) which denigrated their status. While the policeman in the U.K. was addressed as officer, the individual policeman in the country was a minor minion of the law. Orders were issued by the government now to address them as *aap* (plural) but this was meaningless unless specific amelioratives were also taken. A senior British officer (and soon the entire lot of them were to leave the country on the attainment of independence, for careers elsewhere in the empire in colonies and protectorates), was unable to understand the import of the innovation. In the army the jawan was happy to be addressed as *tum* and steeped in the army tradition, he turned round and enquired if the new leaders had ordered the expunction of the word *tum* from the dictionary. This order regarding the form of address was later to result in a police rebellion in 1946. When a magistrate addressed a police constable in his court room as *tum* when the orders were to address them as *aap*, and failed to apologise for his mistake, the constables went on rampage, making various demands including a raise in pay etc. This was really an occasion to re-emphasise the requirements of welfare measures for the police subordinates, which were sorely lacking. The absenting from duty by armed policemen, promptly brought the army into the picture. Conflicts developed and in several sectors the army jawans had to fire on armed policemen, who were divested of the arms given to them for duty. This rebellion could only be controlled with army bayonets and the leader of the movement, an erstwhile police constable who had resigned from the force in 1942 and who was later to become the Home Minister in the state of Bihar, was taken into custody and was detained without trial. He was arrested with great difficulty. Ramanand Tiwari, that was his name, became overnight a leader and the subordinate police looked to him for assistance in all their demands. Tiwari organised a policemen's association for Bihar to which contributions came in from the rank and file despite a government ban on the association and on any contribution to it by government employees. Tiwari's visit to any police station or Lines was banned but this did not deter him and policemen welcomed him with open arms. Senior police officers could get no information regarding the visits. In regard to this rebellion in my district, the constabulary showed remarkable confidence in me. They unhesitatingly asserted that they were prepared to act at my behest as they felt that I would guide them correctly in their in-service or even domestic matters. But they were aware that the government did not have any plan to ameliorate their wretched plight. Their pay scales were most inequitous and though an armed wing of the establishment, there were no welfare schemes for them. This was the same story as in the early part of the year when I was posted temporarily at Patna and the constables had struck work demanding better living conditions. The constables in the metropolis were happy to work under my guidance but had to resort to the extreme step in view of the cussedness of the government. And over this I could have no control. They therefore made a token abstention from duty. This demonstration of personal loyalty had touched me greatly and the same story was repeated in Saharsa. The constables were looking for sympathetic leadership in their superior cadres and not the wooden discipline which had characterised police working so far. Even though the trouble was got over by making various promises, events were later to show that the governmental analysis was far from a realistic appraisal of the situation. The bayonets of the army were helpful only temporarily. Yet the incoming government went on expanding the armed police to control any possible law and order situation. This force consisted greatly of disgruntled elements and added to the unpopularity of the government. All this matched ill with the feeling of the governing group which felt that their strong point was the contact with their own castemen in the constabulary, appealing to their sectarian instincts. The Chief Minister would get in touch with the Bhumihars and the Finance Minister the Rajputs to settle the issues. How could the problem be solved in this manner ? Even the discussions in the cabinet over this issue, were greatly coloured by such considerations. I got to know of it from the constables themselves who were sought to be influenced in this fashion.

At this time, I made a trip to the southern part of the country. I visited Rameshwaram and on the return journey proceeded to Dhanushkodi pier to catch the Indo-Ceylonese Express. We were not allowed to occupy any berth on this train as it was pompously stated that the passengers on the boat from Ceylon had to have priority. Shri Lanka was then known as Ceylon. Why the railways could not obtain advance information of the requirements from the Ceylon end, was not quite clear. Nevertheless, waiting in one of the compartments—as there was no other place on the platformless station, the working booth also was a straw hut—we found the steamer arrive and some of the passengers occupy a few berths on the train. It appeared that we might be cast out quite unnecessarily but espying a railway ticket checking Inspector going about, my wife handed over some currency notes to him asking for reservation and the tickets. The sight of money seems to have activised this underling—he promptly got the tickets and made us comfortable. The change that he got was pocketed by him. I was reminded of another friend who told me that every time he needed a berth on a train at Howrah railway station all he had to do was to press a fiver into the palms of any railway checking staff and that did the trick. These tips were accepted without any fear of check or detection.

The visit of a minister to the district headquarters at this time was of considerable interest and some amusement to the officials who were slowly ganging up as a separate social group even though some of them vied with each other to win favours of these politicians who were going to take charge of affairs. These dignitaries, expected the senior local government officials to receive them on arrival at the station. On one occasion when the seniormost police officer present at the district headquarters was a Deputy Superintendent of Police, the Minister took umbrage at having been offered a salute by the Deputy Superintendent of Police alone, while other members of the police party who were there to receive him, stood at attention. This was an appropriate procedure but it incensed the Minister and he called for the explanation of the Deputy S.P. for not ensuring a salute by the entire police party. When the rules were pointed out to the Minister and he was informed that no discourtesy whatsoever to the dignity of his position could be intended, he promptly quipped on the file that these observations were entirely gratuitous and that he did not feel happy at all the way the salutation had been given to him. The pomposity of the political leadership itching to assume full powers and now claiming special courtesies and salutes was incongruous considering the ideals held up by the Father of the Nation. This was to be the order in the years to follow and was particularly noticeable in the early years of independence. While these leaders demanded liveried attendance by government functionaries it was amusing to find that they did not even know how to answer the salutation. These salutes were the subject of many an interesting cartoon appearing in almost all the newspapers and journals in the country.

The posting and transfer of officers was to become the favourite pastime of the political leaders who had ensconsed themselves in comfortable administrative positions. Party positions were shunned by them but even the smallest job in the government set-up was welcome. Naturally all this aroused sectarian and narrow considerations which did not add a whit to the reputation of the future leaders of the country and the government. It was fantastic that a request should come from one of the ministers to me as a District S.P. to transfer a chowkidar from his village to another. The rural police in the eastern part of India are only part-time employees drawn from the locality and the job was usually kept in the family. There was no question of transferring them as in a large number of cases even land had been bestowed on the families in lieu of service to be rendered by them in the village. This request coming from a minister of the state government who was also a graduate of law, was an astounding instance of ignorance and showed the stuff the leadership was made of. When told that such transfers were not possible, the minister felt annoyed that his instructions had not been carried out by the district administrative officers. A similar episode concerned the grant of a gun licence. A relation of the minister wanted a licence for his gun, the possession of which was considered to be an item of prestige in the countryside. When informed that these licences were granted by the District Magistrate and not by the Superintendent of Police, who had merely to verify the antecedents of the applicant and forward his recommendations, the minister took umbrage and swore that he would settle scores with him in due course. Later under the new dispensation, this political luminary occupied several positions of importance, specially as he was a member of the backward class, though a very rich landlord himself. As a member of the state cabinet in later years, he could not get over his habit of dozing off at all odd occasions. He was interested in establishing the new district headquarters in his home town of Madhipura, then a sub-divisional town. The decision of the Cabinet was to keep the headquarters at Saharsa, where it had been temporarily set up. The minister was dozing off when the matter was discussed by the cabinet. He realised this later and raised some points, which did not cut much ice. He now fostered a movement in the area for reconsideration of the government decision ! On another occasion he sent for me when I was in the midst of an important meeting of the police officers of my district at Patna. I told him that I could go a little later but he wanted my immediate presence. When I met him at his house, all he wanted to know was the detailed crime statistics in the district. While I was busy trying to impress on him the troubles in the countryside engendered by his co-castemen and quoted statistics, I realised to my dismay that the minister was fast asleep. I therefore stopped dead in my dissertation. I noticed some members of the minister's household peeping from behind the curtains. The minister later woke up with a start and came to the point viz. that one of his relations who was living with him required a licence for a revolver. Some of the audience behind the curtains also made themselves visible now. I told the minister that this matter should be referred to the District Magistrate who was competent to deal with it, yet he insisted on my issuing the licence leave aside any question of forwarding any application. When I was in Saharsa this minister was yet a parliamentary secretary. On his arrival at the district headquarters of Saharsa, he had sent me a note bearing the appellation Captain Nath, and asked me to meet him at the railway station. I did go to see him there, when he enquired if I could arrange for some ration supplies for his entourage. However, having told him about the rules for grant of ration cards, which was the work pigeon of the district supply officer, I pointed out that I belonged to the I.P. and was not a Captain of the army. Somewhat earlier another Captain Nath (of the I.M.S.) was Superintendent of the Patna General Hospital and later Superintendent of the Hazaribagh Central Jail. The latter post was filled by I.M.S. officers. Yet this political leader promptly quipped that I could not fool him as he had known of my earlier postings ! The position was too fantastic for words. I had mentioned this episode to the Divisional Commissioner, who later occupied the position of Chief Secretary in the state and other posts in the government of India including that of Health Secretary. The Commissioner told me amidst peals of laughter that he was himself required by this leader to meet him at the Circuit House at Bhagalpur in the early hours of the morning.

On arriving there—he went there after enquiring if the matter was of such importance as to require his immediate presence—he had found the VIP asleep and when he could be roused, he merely asked the Commissioner to let him have a few *seers* (kilos had not been adopted then) of rice for personal consumption. The Commissioner could not avoid expressing his disapproval of the manner in which he was summoned to the august presence, but it had no impression on this rising star of our political firmament. Later when the question had arisen of supplying staff cars to the new Ministers after 1947, this well educated and influential member of the cabinet was also requested to record his preference. State Ministers were given low salaries but a plethora of expensive perquisites including a new car which was run with public funds and for travelling in it the minister drew a fat travelling allowance to boot ! Travelling allowance, which meant a fat monthly income computed in four figures only, did not attract any income-tax and allowed our political leaders to add to their purses. So when this dignitary was required to name his brand of motor vehicle required : some asked for a Dodge, or Chevrolet, but our friend named it as "truck". He had been told by some leg pullers to name this "model" as it was capacious and could take the entire family around. He was apparently unaware that there was no car of this model or make.

The position of senior police officers, squarely responsible for handling the murky political set up, was unstable to a degree and caused considerable unease in the minds of more than one officer. It was too late now to decide to chuck up the job and seek one's fortune in other spheres, as the option allowed earlier had not been availed of by almost all the Indian elements. There was the lingering feeling that prospects outside the service might not be much better. There was also the idea that the reorganisation of this giant machine—the government—may require expert handling and the expertise for it was available with us which should be pumped into the national stream. Even though the picture was gloomy, I had decided to carry on in the I.P. knowing that I may have to fend for myself. I was unable to cast my lot with any small group, which was based on political support. Therefore I could only flounder forward.

6

INDEPENDENCE COMES

THE DAWN of independence on 15 August 1947 saw tumultuous scenes of public exultation all over the country, specially in the provincial capitals where Governor under the new dispensation were sworn in. The government was headed by Chief Ministers, then known as Prime Ministers of states, and the new Governor was to be a virtual figurehead though the trappings of his office continued and he was declared as the dejure head of the state administration. The departure of the British element and also quite a large number of the Muslim officials at the senior levels, left the secretariat in considerable disarray. I was specially selected at this juncture to take command of the Railway Protection Force of the state which was a sprawling organisation. I was told that in determining postings, political and local considerations had played a very important part and that I was placed in this position as it did not involve local patronage. All 'cream' jobs were meant for those only who could exercise some political pull and whose local influence would be helpful for the votes required for the coming elections. This force which I was required to command had a strength of over four thousand armed men, spread over the entire province, for guarding important and bigger railway bridges, and installations. It was a big unit considering that the entire strength of the special armed police in the province was nearly half of this force. The deployment of this sprawling force with hardly any casualty reserve to replace those going on leave etc. was a big headache and I found that I was constantly on the go, visiting units, enthusing them, and lending them help which I could profer. The protection along the railway track had to be foolproof and any mishap would have been squarely fastened on us. I was very unhappy at this assignment, as the armed police set up was very unimaginative with little facilities for the men who were seething with discontent. The recompense was additional pay and the fancied railway saloons without which I could not have moved about chasing my job. These saloons were requisitioned even by the state Prime Minister as getting one from the railways through the normal channels would be a difficult exercise. So far as I was concerned I had to be told that the saloon was required for the big ones and I booked it in my name along certain routes as required. All this irked me greatly and I was happy therefore to be placed on special duty soon after with the new Governor, as his Secretary and major domo par excellence. The earlier incumbents who were Britishers quit in good time before August, 1947. There was no break in the working order in the Governor's establishment : in fact this was a case of new wine in the old bottles, the facade being the same. In sartorial proprieties, the *shirwani* and the *churidar* became the official dress and the other appendages functioned as of yore. At the oath-taking ceremony I had appeared in khaki silk turban, an optional form of headgear laid down for the Imperial Police and particularly designed for Sikh officers. The confusion which broke loose on the occasion of the arrival of the new Governor at the airport to take oath of office did not augur well for the people. The formal parade arranged ended in complete pandemonium. The Governor, (Jairamdas Daulatram) was a seasoned Gandhian and made a very impressive showing at the Government House (now known as Raj Bhawan) function. He told me, however, when I formally joined him that he would like to carry on the traditions of the British Governors : food of the English style was to be served at Raj Bhawan and everyone present had to dress for dinner. When he made a visit immediately after taking office to some remote district headquarters, he carried several changes of clothing so that he could appear immaculately dressed at each function : not quite the wont in Congress circles. There was a string of callers at the Raj Bhawan all anxious to be friendly with me to see that they were well attended to. There were invitations to parties both in and outside Raj Bhawan and these followed earlier lines. Whisky flowed like water, notwithstanding the Congress pledge for non-drinking. Jairamdasji was always anxious that his car should have appropriate pennants and the old vogue in police arrangements should be followed including the lining of routes when he went about the town. All this was now entirely out of place and inappropriate, and I felt considerably amused at the goings on. Was this the independence we were looking for ?

The onrush of displaced persons both from the eastern and western wings of the new Pakistan, resulted in special arrangements being set on foot in India for their reception and rehabilitation. The Rajyapal kindly agreed to make available my services for this work and this was much to my liking. It was peculiar that a police officer should have been selected by the government to do this work. Perhaps the idea was that hailing originally from Punjab (now East Punjab), I would be able to inspire some confidence in the incoming people and most of them were from the Punjab area. Perhaps I could sort out the law and order problem the refugees were likely to pose. I had no office and no funds, even my own salary could not be paid in the absence of proper sanctions. The Finance Department of the State considered a sanction for a mere three-month period adequate ! This department was to go on for at least another decade but the shortsightedness of the pundits in the Secretariat was phenomenal. When funds were asked for and sanctioned, one of the members of the Cabinet—the Revenue Minister—told me that I should get hold of a sizable amount under miscellaneous head and go about distributing it to the needy according to requirement ! This indicated the awareness of the problem and the manner in which it was likely to be tackled. A fairly high level meeting was convened in this connection with the Chief Minister in the chair very much in the style of a durbar. The officers attending this meeting were more anxious to get near the Chief Minister to be able to offer their respects to him by touching his feet rather than face the problem and put up proposals. The chief minister was expected to give the *firman*. But this was not forthcoming. The work was placed in the portfolio of the Public Works Department Minister, a Muslim, and to help him a Parliamentary Secretary was nominated. Naturally the Parliamentary Secretary could not exercise the functions of a Minister or a Deputy Minister unless he was formally given this position. As this was not feasible, the incumbent was known as Parliamentary Secretary in-charge of refugee rehabilitation. He attempted to deal with the connected files directly with the other State government departments, who would not recognise his authority.

On their part the important ministers considered the new refugee settlements, as centres of discontent against the government, and fit to be placed under surveillance of the Special Branch; some others considered that the influx should be stopped completely as there was no scope in the state of Bihar for their rehabilitation. Jairamdas Daulatram, hailing from Sindh, wanted that at least Sindhis should be encouraged to come as they had no place of their own in India while the Punjabis had East Punjab and the Bengalis had West Bengal. He invited regularly to the Raj Bhawan bunches of Sindhi refugees so that they could at least have a decent bath and food, which were not available to them anywhere else. This was a great gesture but was not liked by other denizens of the refugee camp at Patna as they thought they should also be looked after in a similar manner. Many an ugly scene was created in the refugee camp over this issue. Some of the men were rude and rough to the Rajyapal when he visited the camp and it was a job for me to keep tempers even. The common comment, however, was that the refugees appeared to be well off, as they went about better clad than the local crowd. It was not appreciated that the refugees had come away with items that they considered valuable and therefore till these clothes were worn out, they would go about in the best that was available to them in their original homes. In short there was no evidence of any sympathy for the refugees and for me it was a great disappointment as the incoming crowd placed their faith in me. The Government of India brochures on refugee rehabilitation work prominently featured the camps that I was organizing. Doubtless I had set the state scheme going effectively in spite of the shortsighted approach of the local administration. I had to set up the office of the new department under canvas in the compound of the Secretariat building, which was by all standards an elegant edifice. The stepmotherly treatment accorded was evidenced from the fact that the available space on the overbridge connecting two wings of this building was later pigeonholed to accommodate us. This was indeed a poor recompense for all the earnestness and enthusiasm that was put in to get things going. To add to the confusion the Parliamentary Secretary, who was dejure not competent to take any decisions or to pass an order, continued to go on and even attended the coordination meetings at the central level. He was cold shouldered, and felt very unhappy. He was elevated later to the rank of a Deputy Minister attached to the Chief Minister and this proved helpful. But all this was a slow process. I learnt, however, that the promotion to this politician was not given earlier as his son was a prominent member of the Communist Party of India.

I can recall vividly my visit to a refugee camp at Ghatshila, near the steel city of Jamshedpur. The camp was located on the deserted runway and abandoned hutments of a war-time air base. The poor refugees, who were huddled there, under canvas or temporary hutments, found that they had been dropped out of the blue with no chance of local rehabilitation. They wanted some position nearer Jamshedpur but the government was not willing to allow this. The matter was further complicated when a good chunk of East Bengal refugees also started coming here. There would be collisions between the refugees hailing from the eastern and the western sectors of the country. The eastern sector people were easy going and content with the doles but the westerners would slip away, whenever the slightest chance arose, to Jamshedpur to earn and stand on their own feet. I had in fact gone to fix up a schedule for this movement which I had found the district administration unwilling to agree to. The camp commandant, a member of the state subordinate civil service and a college friend, came up to me wanting to be spared from this assignment which placed him in uncongenial surroundings. While I sympathised with this officer I felt that young officers should work with a missionary zeal notwithstanding the fact that the officer's family lacked company of their own sort and some other conveniences normally available at other stations in conventional jobs. The junior officers merely looked at a posting from the angle of promotion and avenues of social advancement. This attitude of the public servant had to change. For the displaced persons there was no solace, yet hats off to the people coming from the west, who probed into the nearest marketing centres and started peddling wares which were an improvement on the stuff that was available locally. They made a niche for themselves, in spite of official apathy. In Patna, the state capital, small shops with corrugated iron sheet partitions were set up near the railway station on a vacant piece of land. These shops did roaring business and those who occupied them were soon to become affluent, much to the chagrin of local shopkeepers whose business methods were so crude and archaic that they lost in the race. A *kirana* shop started there, has now proliferated into a departmental store and a provision store with branches all over the city, which is the envy of local businessmen.

A conference of state representatives in charge of rehabilitation was convened at Delhi about this time. This conference was inaugurated by the Prime Minister. I had a very close look at Jawaharlal Nehru at this function. He was also new to the Central Secretariat building and confessed that unchaperoned, he would lose his way in it. The Parliamentary Secretary, in charge of rehabilitation work of my state actually went down a wrong staircase and could be located with some difficulty. I found that there was not much verve in the official programme for rehabilitation, as the government was busy with other problems of Partition. There was no control room and no expertise was in evidence in getting down to business even at the centre. This was a great damper to my enthusiasm and only buttressed my feeling that I should go back to a police job—which materialised quickly.

Back in the Police, I found the department ruling the roost. The special branch was keeping tabs on the likely agitators which included even displaced persons with whom I had been dealing so far. But local patronage and casteism had penetrated in a big way. The junior elements in the state police service failing in their attempt to disrupt the seniority code which favoured the direct recruits, were trying to get their proteges placed in positions so that the police chief's actions (he was a Muslim) were constantly monitored. That gave them a feeling of importance. The I.G.'s forte was for getting things done and it suited him to have this host of officers taking his load off. The Chief Minister, in the Machiavellian style which was peculiar to his caste block, would lead the I.G. to actions which had been approved by the caucus round him. When certain appointments and promotions were desired by this group, the C.M. would quietly request the police chief indicating his personal interest and the I.G. acquiesced in it. The prospects were not good in the Police Department also but some effective work appeared feasible.

It was apparent that in the exuberance of the newly found independence, the people in the countryside were losing their sense of discipline, and this made it necessary to deploy larger and larger bodies of police to control minor situations. All the ministers, however, were happy in the display of this force, posses of which accompanied them here and there. It greatly helped in boosting their ego. There was a large expansion of the armed police, therefore and units of the State armed police reserves also proliferated. These units could now be positioned whenever a situation arose for which initially in 1947, the army assistance was taken. But that was little recompense to the tax payer, who wanted better police service, effective in enabling him to carry on his avocation in life This was not in evidence. Only there were larger allocations for the police and new taxes were being levied. As for the police, their deployment now was considered in terms of sections, when previously only one or two armed constables would have been adequate. In the post 1942 period, the danger of internal uprising had made the British rulers strengthen armed police posts. The new rulers did not know how to cut down on this. The senior police echelons also failed to advise the government on the point ; perhaps they found that their own positions would be firmly fixed if government dependence on the armed police went on increasing. Armed men now symbolised the police which was not so earlier. They would fire at the slightest provocation making the department more vulnerable to public criticism.

Rather than raise a separate force, a new organisation—the Home Guards—was brought into being as a wing of the police department. The idea was also to enthuse the people in the country and discipline them. It would also be possible to utilise the services of the Home Guards as part-time policemen to reduce the pressure on the police proper. But the organisation was captained in such an unskilled manner that the action became counter productive. The Home Guards organisation provided important scandals of the state administration. The military (armed) police which was also expanded simultaneously got into a similar jam though this was less so as it consisted entirely of stipendiary incumbents, which the Home Guards were not.

It would be interesting to indicate how the Home Guards were organised. In the villages and in the urban areas, young men of the age group 20-35 years were specially selected, given a brief course of discipline and some military type of training, and were then placed on a list for being called out for duty periodically to aid the police and also to take up civil defence chores. They were trained in field parade of the police variety, in extinguishing fires and in First Aid. Rather than leaven the morale in the countryside, the incumbents became a cadre of inferior policemen for manning various posts for which the normal armed police was not available. The organisation also became the preserve of a group in the politics of the state, and was utilised for personal propaganda in the countryside. A group of this nature could not rise to the occasion ever. There was no attempt also at broadbasing selection techniques so as to have a sample of the state population in it. The Home Guards therefore continued to make a poor showing and practically failed in achieving the goals which were set.

Having been spared from the rehabilitation department, I was placed in charge of the military police units in the state, a job which again like the Railway Protection Force which I was required to head earlier, did not have any patronage of the type which attracted local incumbents. My headquarters were near Dalmianagar, a sizeable industrial township. There was a big fire in a paper manufacturing factory near the headquarters of my unit. The damage was to the tune of several lakhs of rupees. The fire could only be extinguished with the aid of the fire brigade called in from distant sectors. The military police also worked in a big way to help extinguish the fire but it was not possible for them to function in the way the fire brigade could do particularly because the appliances connected with this work were not available. I was required to take full charge of the situation even though I had no legal authority to do so, this being the job of the District Police Superintendent. I indicated this to the Chief Secretary, who rang me up about it. The result, the rules were amended to enable the commandants of military police units to have local authority. When I had pointed it out in the beginning to the Chief Secretary, my views were not palatable. The Chief Secretary was merely trying to exercise the authority that had been newly vested in him much earlier than he could have dreamt of. This incident led to a visit by the Inspector General to go into the problem. The officers of the district administration also came into the picture. I found that this was not a case of tackling the problem, but of getting into the favours of the political bosses and their hand-maidens the secretariat brass, particularly the Chief Secretary. The Durbar style was apparent and it was more manifest when the Chief Minister visited my headquarters to assess the effectiveness of the military police organisation : a question which was raised after this fire. When he arrived with his entourage, the I.G. and other senior officers were anxious only to minister to his personal comforts. These officers even prided on peeping through bathroom keyholes to determine the state of the VIP's preparedness for the day's engagements. I had to entertain the Chief Minister and his hangers-on to a meal, which went off very well. This was at the beginning of the day. The Chief motored through the camp and that was all. He had no experience to be able to make any worthwhile suggestion nor did his health permit him being a chronic diabetic. Despite this, however, he relished chicken and pudding even at breakfast.

About this time, I paid a visit to Ranchi, where I met a *tantric*, who was the ruling deity in the state. By his special planchette, he arranged for Chief Minister to communicate with the soul of his deceased wife. Almost the entire cabinet was under his thumb ; no wonder that police officers of various religious faiths, were also with him. He would obtain messages for them from their departed relations, and some of these touched the routine work of the department like postings, transfers and promotion. I was lucky to get a sitting with him but I was much disappointed at the result. He wanted to establish my contact with my late sister's soul but the incoherent responses showed that perhaps he had little knowledge of my family background. Later this *tantric* was involved in bacchanalian orgies including an escapade with a refugee girl from Dacca, whom he ultimately married.

I was soon to be placed in charge of police work in an important district in the state, Dhanbad. This district contained almost all the coal mines in the state and had several other industries besides. The foreign elements still had an important say in the coal industry, and even the old chief inspector of mines, a Britisher, continued to function. The local Gymkhana Club provided for the admission of only two or three Indians to the club. The Deputy Commissioner and the Superintendent of Police, kingpins of the administration, were invited to join, but not any one else. A retired High Court judge presided over the labour tribunal and a retired civil service officer was managing the coal mines welfare fund, but neither was given a place in the club. There was considerable controversy and even some talk of this and other similar gymkhana clubs being wound up. In their place new station clubs were being started with provision for taking in the local Indian elite. A new station club was opened at Dhanbad in the neighbourhood of the gymkhana club, but it did not gather momentum then. I believe now both the clubs are running concerns and the gymkhana club has lost all its glamour. VIPs both from the state capital and Delhi made frequent visits to this place. The unprecedented dry spell had at this time caused considerable hardship and an organisation for coordination and collation of relief work was set up on an all-India level. The visit of Dr. Rajendra Prasad, President of this Relief Committee, for collection of funds was an important event. The local bigwigs made their contributions in terms of a few thousand rupees, but the target was fairly high as Dhanbad area was considered a gold mine. The collection being much below the expected level, Dr. Rajendra Prasad was dismayed, but was happy when one of the mine magnates, Wali Ram Taneja rose in his seat at the meeting and offered to make up the deficit without wasting valuable time on this work. He requested Rajendra Babu to keep to his other engagements. Though generally decrying the titles which were now not in vogue, Rajendra Babu averred that Wali Ram Taneja was truly a Bahadur and a Dewan (holder of funds)—the Dewan Bahadur title was well deserved and apt so far as he was concerned. Dewan Bahadur Wali Ram Taneja, starting as a petty coal merchant, had built up an empire and endowed a trust to protect cows from being butchered. He set up a Goshala by purchasing the entire lot of about two hundred cows being taken to an abbattoir in the Calcutta area. The trust organised schools and conducted other charitable works, but it was sad that earlier he was branded as an R.S.S. supporter and was detained in 1948 after the assassination of Mahatma Gandhi. Undeterred he had given all assistance to the ruling Congress party in organising relief etc. and thus improving their image in the countryside. He was released from detention just before I joined as District Superintendent at Dhanbad. The churlish manner in which the local administrative machinery led by the Congress worked did not add to their reputation or popularity. Yet at this stage no other political party could be thought of and even the Socialists were keeping on mainly as a part of the Congress. This monolith ruled the country for three decades.

The Deputy Commissioner, who was an officer promoted from the state civil service, was well known for his antics. He would enjoy his mid-day siesta ordering the peon on duty not to disturb him unless the caller was his boss, the Divisional Commissioner. One day the Chief Secretary rang up the Deputy Commissioner at his house, but the peon refused to rouse his boss from his siesta. The Deputy Commissioner having woken up accidentally came to the telephone and when he was told by the Chief Secretary that the peon would not call him to the phone, this officer promptly upbraided the peon while the phone call was on, little realising that this would be heard on the other side. He told the peon that he had ordered to be roused if the Divisional Commissioner called and the peon should realise that the present caller, the Chief Secretary, was the *baap* of the Commissioner ! The incident showed the style of functioning of the administration. The same Deputy Commissioner, got so nervous on the occasion of the arrival of one of the central ministers that he introduced the officials on the platform, giving a wrong name in each case. The officers were embarrassed. Later when I told the Deputy Commissioner of the mistakes committed, he averred that it made no difference as the VIP presumably did not know any of the waiting officials by name.

An interesting episode was the visit by the State Minister for public health engineering projects, who specially came along as he wanted to show round the new Secretary of his department (an ICS officer) the position in situ ! This Minister also presided over the send off ceremony for the Public Health Engineer who was migrating to Australia. Undeterred the Minister offered to keep on this engineer, even though he had already handed over charge ! This engineer had no special qualifications for the job, but his trump card was that he always kow-towed to the Minister and introduced him as a fine specimen of a public leader, who was a Bachelor of Science as well and therefore needed no explanation and elucidation of the engineering projects due to his scientific knowledge ! The Minister enjoyed the encomiums from this foreigner ; he expressed his approbation by twirling his moustaches, and he had a fine pair of these. This was the standard of Ministers who had come to power in the state. As to the ineptitude of the ministers, the stories going the rounds hardly did justice to them. Shah Ozair Munimi, a devout Muslim and an Urdu scholar had several important departments of the government in his portfolio. He had a personal antipathy for one of the departmental secretaries. When he did not like the notes of the Secretary in a file, he recorded that "the Secretary is warned." It meant perhaps that the Secretary should record his notes carefully as according to him some aspects of the case had not been covered by the officer. This officer took umbrage at such notes by the Minister and referred the file to the Chief Minister for reconsideration of the matter. The Chief Minister indicated that warnings could be recorded only after detailed examination of the case and not casually. The Minister, construed it to mean that casual warning was not appropriate. He, therefore, recorded that he had "warned the Secretary perpetually"—he meant always. All these notes were later expunged from the file. This same Minister was credited with having showed his importance to his wife by telling her that he could put her directly on the phone with the state Governor ! No wonder Winston Churchill had designated these persons as "men of chaff".

The list of VIPs was now legion. And they competed with each other as to who enjoyed more elaborate security arrangements and police fanfare including the blowing of the bugle when the police guard of honour was presented. The brief period of about two years after independence had resulted in finalising a blue-book of instructions regarding the security arrangements for some VIPs, which I was aghast to find were much more elaborate than those in vogue in the earlier regime, when attacks on those in authority were possible due to the unpopularity of the administration. That the leaders, elected by popular vote, should consider such arrangements necessary showed the egoism which had swamped this corps of elites. The arrangements consisted of forming an obtrusive ring with uniformed men and an unobtrusive plain clothes staff ring also, with whistling policemen in uniform controlling the movement of the VIPs motorcade through the crowded streets. There was stoppage of traffic for long periods, much to the annoyance of the road user. In some cases the housetops alongside the road were carefully watched and guarded. This was not understood by the people and added nothing to the popularity of these "popular" leaders. When the VIP moved round in urban areas in a car it was customary to have a posse of armed men go in front in a pilot vehicle with a fluttering flag. The VIP's entourage very often took advantage of a free ride. The new VIPs seemed to delight in all this pomp and show.

A new police office building came up in Dhanbad; previously the office was accommodated in a few rooms of the local police station building. When I wanted this new office to be modernized, I was told that this was useless and all that was required was to get on with the same old equipment. I was astounded at this attitude.

I found the state of affairs in the local jail located in the neighbourhood shocking as it functioned as a subdivisional prison though Dhanbad was a District headquarters. When I reported about it, I was told that the Inspector General of Prisons would make an inspection in due course and settle the issue. To my consternation, I found the Law Secretary to Government, an I.C.S. officer, come along to make the inspection as the Law department was the custodian of the prisons as well. This officer informed me that he was inspecting all jails in the state : even though the Inspector General of Prisons, an I.M.S. officer, was expected to do this work! Apparently, the I.C.S. officer was making these visits with the intention of denigrating the I.M.S. officer. Now the all-India services were not working with the amity and cooperation which had been their hallmark in the pre-1947 period. I wondered what would happen if the Secretary of Home Department (the Chief Secretary was the Home Secretary also) started inspecting District Police offices. I for one would not have allowed him to do so as the police operated under the orders of the I.G. It was for the I.G. to determine when and how to get orders of government. A Secretary to government had not the locus standi to make any inspection of subordinate executive units.

The state of police buildings in the state was pitiable. In my earlier charge in Saharsa, I had the mortification of seeing a police station function from a door-less, window-less relic of a railway station building, that was in use when some rail lines existed in the Kosi belt. There was tall elephant grass growing all round the P.S. building and the lot of the officer posted here could only be termed miserable. Yet another police station, located in the village near the ancestral home of L.N. Misra later to become a central minister, was housed in straw huts, with the height of the eaves barely four feet from the ground. In all these posts the police lock-up contraption was to chain the person arrested to available tables and benches. In the case of the dis-used railway station building, the prisoner was tied to large rings driven into the wall of the building. Even in the capital town of the province, the lock-up room also housed the urinal and for the purpose of this easement, a pot was sometimes provided which remained inside the lock-up room and had to be taken out by the occupants themselves to be dumped into a neighbouring open drain. However, I found in neighbouring U.P., in the districts adjoining Bihar, that each police station was like a mini fort with an armed sentry at the main entrance. The position in Punjab was a step forward and it appeared to be a real post of occupation of the countryside. But in Bihar where the conditions appeared to be more settled, the P.S. buildings were little better than a block of barrack rooms. After 1942, there was a move to standardise police station buildings and designs were prepared accordingly. These had provision for battlements on the roof, for protection against a surprise attack. I felt that it was time, the buildings of the basic police functions i.e. the police station, received attention. These should provide for waiting halls, complaint counters and such other items. However, it was indeed an idle dream. These projects were not being considered as the police were taken for granted in all their functions. I considered that the lock up system should be reviewed but I was told that this idea was impracticable and utopian. Even lavatory and urinal for undertrial prisoners in the lock-ups in courts could not be provided !

The normal functioning of the administration involved the use of a secret code for conveying messages of a top-secret nature from the state headquarters to the executive echelons in the districts. This code was rarely used in the past but with the coming in of the new dispensation, it was interesting to find a constant string of messages in code sent down even on trivial matters. The plea taken was that some exercise in coding and decoding of messages would be useful. The code was available only to the district officer and the District Superintendent of Police, and the district officer generally relied for this work on the District Superintendent of Police. The incumbent in Dhanbad found himself in difficulties when a message was received by him in code in my absence from the district headquarters, as he had forgotten the code word that he should have memorised. He was sure that the message was regarding some routine matter but was anxious to know what it was all about. Failing in his endeavours to decode the message, he, with some difficulty, established contact with the District Superintendent of a neighbouring district on the telephone. He did not like to contact the district officer as he might then lose face. He was indeed happy to make the contact and then he enquired from the S.P. if a similar message had been received at his end also. Being told that this was not so, he wanted to have the code word passed on to him on the long distance phone. The Superintendent of

Police was unable to disclose this information but the District Magistrate now requested him to relay it in a soft voice so that it could not be overheard ! Earlier there was another interesting incident in relation to the decoding of messages when I was posted as Superintendent in the district of Saharsa. The District Magistrate of neighbouring Darbhanga, received a coded message and as usual finding it difficult to decode, he telephoned the District Superintendent to kindly come to his residence. He also informed him that *khana* was ready. As it was near dinner time, the S.P. construed it to mean that the district officer would like him to take pot-luck with him. On reaching the District Magistrate's house the S.P. was shown into the office room where he was joined by the District Magistrate, the latter having a *pan* in his mouth. It was then the S.P. realised that *khana* (the District Magistrate hailed from Bengal) meant the squared matrix which was necessary for decoding messages, and not the dinner, that he had looked forward to !

Barely two years after independence the stratification of the disciplined police in caste groups was evident. The executive magistrates had necessarily to follow the same pattern. Result : the anti-social elements belonging to the dominating caste group, got out of hand as they had the support and protection of their own caste men. Some of these groups formed into dacoit gangs. The problem of dacoity therefore assumed larger proportions and was difficult to tackle. This was to pose a bigger problem in the years to come. The problem of corruption was also looming large with groupism in political, social, administrative, and even in the educational and developmental spheres. The political leaders were, however, smug in the feeling that with caste support their position would remain unassailed. As for the labour front, the leaders had a special importance in the industrial belt. It was common knowledge that most of them, professing to espouse the cause of the wage earner, were themselves living in luxurious style in airconditioned apartments, when airconditioning had not been adopted in a big way at all. And their families spent most of the time in the cool comfort of the hills in summer and in the holiday resorts in the winter months along the seashore. They were known to have expensive habits which were sustained only by contributions received from the small industrialists, afraid of agitation by the labour. This fraternity could continue their stream of earnings provided they kept the labour leaders happy with appropriate contribution for their household expenses. With all these developments, anti-corruption was important but the newly created department concentrated more on the subordinates, who could obtain small tips that hardly required the attention of a centralised organisation. I started examining the issue in depth to assail it at the most vulnerable point. There was at that time a check post in the district on the borders of West Bengal which was expected to exercise vigilance over the movement of foodgrains and some other items across the border as laid down by the rules. This check post and similar ones in other parts of the state, were hot-beds of corruption but it was impossible to proceed against them in view of the lukewarm attitude of the supervisors located in the Secretariat at Patna. I attempted to form a vigilance cell of my own to do this work. One of the raids made succeeded admirably and the officer of the anti-smuggling force posted on the border of the District, was trapped. Raids such as this involved legal complications. The raiding party had to mingle with the people conveying contraband and had to offer bribes for which, if unsuccessful, they could be arraigned in a law court, as also for attempted smuggling. On one occasion the information about the raid had leaked out, and the officer concerned ran the risk of being mauled by the anti-smuggling staff on whom the trap was laid. He managed to escape by the skin of his teeth. This was indeed a type of work in which the district police force should not have been involved. The work of raids etc. should necessarily have been the duty of the special enforcement agency. The Transport and Development Minister, Dr. Syed Mahmud, an old and veteran freedom fighter and a contemporary of Prime Minister Jawaharlal Nehru during his school and college career, visited Dhanbad. He complained that mobile vigilance units set up for checking corruption and other malpractices indulged in by transport operators, had themselves become corrupt. The mobile vans were painted red. I suggested that now a blue van unit should be set up to check up on the red vans! However, the administrative indifference displayed over the control or containment of this evil was depressing. The Prime Minister even stated that the question should not be brought up in public forums so as to keep up the image of the country's administration abroad. It was little consolation to be told that corruption in public life was an international phenomenon, when we had placed our faith in Gandhian ideals. Gandhiji had been assassinated earlier but we still swore that the path shown by the Father of the Nation, would be our guide. These pious resolutions were apparently giving way to opportunism and selfishness.

I was now posted to the H.Q. of the state as A.I.G. This officer was the principal staff officer of the I.G. and bore the brunt of the work while the police chief busied himself in inspections or policy discussions. The Dhanbad people wanted the government to let me continue there but they were informed that the transfer was a part of the chain of my advancement in my career. Therefore the Dhanbadians desisted from pursuing their earlier stand. Dhanbad was the preserve of the Britisher in the pre-1947 period and my predecessor, an officer promoted from the rank of Sub-Inspector and on the verge of retirement, made no impact. He was placed here more as the last kick up for him before his retirement and particularly because he was friendly with the famous *tantric*, with whom he could arrange interviews for the high-ups. My brief tenure here was therefore generally appreciated. The Dhanbad people gave me a touching farewell even though my contact with them was for a short period.

7

POLICE HEADQUARTERS

THE POLICE force was in need of urgent reorganisation, but it was obvious that the old system had gone so deep into the processes of thinking that changes could not even be conceived of. The apprehension was that such a move may mean a complete tearing up of the fabric of administration. For example, the District police headquarters was run as an army camp, and the ministerial set up was rudimentary and worthless with no public relations outfit. Not only was it necessary to modernise the service-organisation and to provide new equipment, but even small items like the uniform, which had not been changed, required to be gone into. In the field of operations, the old methods were inapplicable, because of the general lack of discipline in the country. It was customary in the pre-independence period for armed police parties to be provided at as many points as possible during religious festivals and these occasions were used by the government for developing sectionalism and schism. Yet these armed forces were now used in greater strength and with a bravado, which added to the load and increased tensions. The festival should have had to larger fraternisation of the religious communities, specially as the country was organised on secular lines and the civilians should have policed the religious events through their own voluntary organisations. But this was not done. Another interesting manifestation was the development plans of the country which went ahead, but the police was completely removed from the ambit of these schemes. The police now constituted a routine expenditure of the non-plan category for which no development plans were considered necessary.

In my old district of Dhanbad the first fertilizer project of the country was coming up at Sindri and it was clear that this would pose a set of police problems. Yet the proposal for planning a police set up in the area went completely by default. Added to it was the picture of the politicians trying to make good in as short a period of time as possible. The result was corruption at the highest levels. The establishment's bugbear was the fear that the administration would crack up if an opposition was allowed to develop. Therefore, big landlords, industrialists, and business tycoons continued to hold their sway though the bulk of the people in the political arena were drawn from the poorer sections of the community. They were in no mood to allow themselves to be displaced from their advantageous positions. Many played an important part in all elections now whether for the constituted legislative bodies, local bodies, or even party posts. The lower rungs of the political cadres went all out to influence the administration ; this brought them financial gains. This was apparent in even small matters like checking of transport vehicles, performance of routine patrols by policemen etc. and this was not unbeknown to the higher political authorities. Earlier the reins of authority had rested with the administrative cadres which meant the officials, but the centre of authority had now shifted to the second or third line politician who had easy access to top echelons in the government and could influence them much as the officials could do in the earlier regime. I would like to mention the case of a Sergeant in the department who was considered quite incompetent during the pre-independence period. He was suspended for irresponsible action but, having resigned from the department he had made his way up in the political world. He ensconced himself in the favour of the top politicians and in fact became their mentor. He became the Chief Minister's personal assistant for security. He would carry tales to the top political echelons, resulting in the senior police officers being isolated. The lower rungs of the police thus completely lost faith in the higher ranks, who were considered to be ineffective. Possibly conditions in the central sphere were to some extent better but the same procedures applied there.

At the police headquarters I wished to make an impact on all these questions. The antiquated police patrol in urban areas based on the system introduced by Walter Swain, one time I.G.P. in the State, continued and needed drastic reforms. I wanted that constables should proceed in two along certain beats, signing registers at specified points and police pill boxes could be set up in towns.

This innovation had no support. Even these patrols were hardly served as police constables were increasingly used in connection with the visits of the VIPs and in tackling labour or student unrest. The crime investigators, Sub-Inspectors of police, had no time for the work. They spent their energy currying favour with politicians and attending to miscellaneous works which were not strictly speaking within the purview of the police department, like looking after school examinations. The result was that cases of dacoity, robbery, and burglary were not recorded and even when this was done, the investigation was so inept that no clue could possibly be found. In such cases a host of arrests were made to create an impression of activity, and later the arrested persons were let off for various considerations including the *pairvi* of powerful politicians or their hangers on. The percentage of cases which were declared as solved would be in the neighbourhood of twenty five but in more than seventy per cent of such cases, the culprits were named and the investigation was merely a case of completing the records to place the matter before a court of law. The possibility of a case involving unknown accused being detected was not more than about five per cent. The courts insisted on a high standard of evidence. With the record of investigation generally poorly made, the acquittals were high, despite executive control of the trying Magistrates. Therefore the final conviction rate achieved was not very much more than about two per cent of the total number of cases reported to and recorded by the police. The impact on law detractors, was therefore minimal. Generally the trial of cases took a long time and the sentence awarded became ineffective. The jails remained crowded with persons of whom a large proportion were undertrials or those who had no charge-sheet given to them. A considerable number arrested were later released for lack of evidence, which showed the levity with which arrests were made. The Criminal Procedure Code allowed detention on suspicion or when the person to be arrested was allegedly moving suspiciously. In such cases the ultimate detention etc. would have been for a period of six months or so, but the trials in some of these cases lasted for years, during which period the arrested person remained in jail as there was no suitable bailer available. The general picture was that of justice delayed and its impression on the people was disastrous so far as the establishment was concerned. The British dispensation did not attempt to improve on it as it suited them in more ways than one. I thought that I might be able to contribute my mite from the police headquarters of the State in tackling these problems as not much financial outlay was involved. But I was dismayed to find that the police department had lost its credibility due to groupism at the top levels and therefore the department's proposals got completely bogged down in the procedural jungle of the Secretariat files.

The first item which I could finalise, was the question of introducing a women's police cadre. The idea was attractive to the top police formations as this would possibly provide domestic help in their households at State expenditure ! This innovation was introduced but with such a mental frame it proved ineffective and was the subject of bitter public criticism. Another question was of transfers and promotions. The Office of the I.G. was responsible for arranging the transfers of gazetted police officers from the rank of Deputy Superintendent of Police upwards. For this job the services of a Deputy Inspector General were being utilised now, but it had been the A.I.G.'s job earlier. This Deputy I.G. had been inducted to keep tabs on the working of his own boss as well ! The departmental selection boards for promotion of non-gazetted officers showed the caste ramifications of the department. And I had to face it all as the Deputy Inspector General arranged to have himself sent out on deputation for a minor course of training at Scotland Yard. I found signs of serious wrangling at the top, which made it a most difficult exercise requiring adjustments and compromise. It was obvious that the procedures adopted earlier were proving inadequate and were inappropriate in the changed climate. Interestingly enough, the Deputy I.G., apprehending that his deputation to the course of training might mean his displacement from his key job, hastened to get back. And this took the headache off so far as I was concerned.

Police parades, earlier an annual feature, became more frequent and were now held sometimes for distributing awards but more often for honouring the innumerable VIPs. These were occasions for speech making, like political gatherings. The departmental chief and the political leader both made speeches, replete with exhortations. The Chief Minister's parades were important as he was the effective head of government. The Rajyapal was relegated to the background and even senior police officials, previously interviewing the Governor regularly for exchange of views, had now to have the CM's sanction before doing so. At the police headquarters, it was my privilege to prepare drafts of speeches for the chief. As he knew Urdu, the speech, which had to be in Hindi the official state language, had to be prepared by me in the Urdu script. The difficulty in reading this with proper emphasis and pronunciation was obvious and added to the amusement of the people.

The police department continued to hold responsibility for the Home Guards and even the fire services. Fire services, in fact, had not developed adequately in the state. It was my privilege to prepare a complete manual of regulations for a reorganised fire service for the state. I prepared these in cooperation with the West Bengal Fire Service Chief. These rules, not very bulky, remained in the archives of the department and the State Secretariat for well over two decades and could not be finalised. Here was an eminent example of the lethargy of the administration and its working where nobody would take any decision and would let things go forward with their earlier momentum.

The general picture of the efficiency of the police at all levels had slumped fast during the early years of independence but the average man in the street did not realise what had happened, as he found the old procedures continuing to rule. The people in general however, appeared to act arbitrarily as they found the police somehow become more ineffective and they ascribed it to local interference. The political workers could now use the police for personal advantage as was not the case earlier. If the police did not play to their tune, the officers concerned could be displaced giving place to the more amenable incumbents. Service, which in the local language was called *chakri*, was indeed now a case of dancing to the tune of the powerful ones, which had nothing to do with legal proprieties. *Chakar hai to nachakar, na nache to na chakar*—this was the refrain. The couplet translated in English meant : If you must serve, dance to the tune of the powers, or else you will be dismissed from service. I realised this fully at the nerve centre of the police department.

As a junior officer, I was not expected to visit the state police headquarters unless sent for but the corridors of the office now often overflowed with visiting officers of all ranks, who tried to push forward their cases. The accepted norm was that you either push your case personally or get a patron to do it or else you would be mulcted of your deserts. Even the office assistants worked in groups spreading tales against the opposing faction. Files started disappearing and little control was possible. It was stated that at the residence of the Minister, bundles of unwanted files were stacked on almirah tops to gather dust. The administration would indeed go on even if no decisions were taken on these files. And orders could be passed nevertheless.

At this stage when the plans for a new police force should have been well on way to realisation, the way work was done can be gauged from the work-routine of the head of the force, which was to attend office for a brief while, during which the formality of signing a few letters had to be gone through and sometimes an interview was granted to a subordinate. This was followed by a visit to the wing which housed the ministry, known locally as the Secretariat department to chat away with a few senior officers. Depressing indeed.

About this time there was a visit by the central Home Minister which, I was informed, was the result of consistent criticism appearing in the local press about the doings of the Ministers and their connections with various scandals including the well known molasses scandal in which a huge quantity of molasses thrown out by the sugar mills was allotted to proteges at throw-away prices, merely to be passed on in turn to distilleries, where they were needed and for which a fancy price was paid. It was merely a case of passing on the licence and making a big packet in the process. The role of the Excise Department here which dealt with molasses was a dubious one. Then there was the scandal publicized in the local papers in which huge bits of good land were settled on agnates of the favoured group in the ministry. The "erring" editor got a dressing down from the Home Minister no less. He was also accused of trying to denigrate his own partymen. The warning went home and the local nationalist press, suddenly ceased to be critical. One learnt that another important factor which helped this was the passing on of a large chunk of land to the editor, who was otherwise in a rather impecunious state. A large chunk of government land was at this time given away as a wedding gift to the daughter of a friend of the Chief Minister. The Sathi land scandal featured in the press and was brought up in the courts also. The old guard in the bureaucracy, could do nothing about it.

The badges of rank, were an important component of police formations particularly because the force had been fashioned on the lines of the land army. The I.G. wore badges of the rank of a Colonel in the army in the old days when the police force in each province was numerically not so large. Later this was upgraded to that of a Brigadier's badge and now in the wake of independence and the extraordinary expansion of armed police in each state, the I.G.'s badge resembled that of a Major General. Presently some of the Unit heads have badges of rank like that of a Lt. General. The District S.P. with responsibility of a very high order, had earlier carried the badges of rank resembling a Captain and was popularly known as the Police Captan. This hardly did justice to this officer. Now the badges like that of a full Colonel were used and that is perhaps nearer the level of his responsibility. However the Police I.G., was always known as General Saheb. Now there was some talk about completely doing away with police badges of rank and to convert the force into a civil formation. At least police work above a certain level could be conducted without uniform like the Customs and Central Excise. The armed part would no doubt have its own nomenclature and grading and be separated from the civil group. Suggestions to this effect were brushed aside as impracticable and a large fraction of the officers themselves desired to carry uniforms to impress the countryside with their importance. The political bosses also wanted the uniformed police to continue to minister to them. Therefore, this question did not make any progress towards solution.

Having been at the State police headquarters for a few months' only, I was now tipped to take charge of the headquarters district of the state, which interestingly went without a substantive officer for a long period due to the difficulty in finding an appropriate incumbent. I was surprised that I should be specially selected for this assignment as I did not bear the mark of any coterie in the police force. It appeared that an experiment was to be made by placing a non-group officer in this position. Also at the police headquarters, it was felt that I was too independent to suit the climate. The Deputy Inspector General posted there wanted a more pliant incumbent. I learnt later that this petty question of posting a Senior Superintendent of Police incharge of the Headquarters District of the state, was discussed in several meetings of the State Cabinet. In the police department and its counterpart in the Secretariat department, the subject was kept on the boil for quite a long time. In the new position that I would fill, the earlier incumbents had come in with some fanfare, but I felt that I was being pushed out of the police headquarters. The reward was the satrapy of a district, as if I had been elevated to a Subedarship in the Mughal dispensation. I was aware of the disabilities of the job ; placed in my care were subordinate officers, who were all the proteges of some one or other of consequence whose doings I would have to tolerate rather than be able to guide them on to their appropriate chores. It would be the case of a higgledy piggledy group, that had to produce an orchestra of sorts.

Soon after assuming charge an interesting case of defalcation in the local District Board was reported. The Chairman of the District Board was a confidante of the ruling clique. This Board interestingly enough was running a local light railway system, which had been taken over due to mismanagement by the company concerned. The founts of the trouble were obvious and I set down to uncovering the misdeeds of the top political brass of the district who were also in control of the District Board. However, this case was taken off the district police and was entrusted to the Criminal Investigation Department. The Chairman of the District Board, who was involved in the case, continued to enjoy all the privileges and his position in the administrative hierarchy (he was also the District Public Prosecutor) remained intact. Sometime later he made his way even into the State Cabinet.

I found that a not-so-young officer of the new I.P.S.—this service was ushered in as a successor to the I.P. like the I.A.S. did for the I.C.S.—was posted as an Assistant Superintendent of Police in the district. This officer had earlier served in the state junior civil service as a Sales Tax Officer. I was mortified to find that a case was launched against this A.S.P. by a Sub-Inspector for alleged misbehaviour. Taking refuge under an enactment which laid down that no action could be taken or proceedings initiated against an officer for acts done in pursuance of his charter of work or under colour of his office, this officer wanted the case to be dropped. He was keeping in touch with the senior officers at police headquarters who were his caste-men and distantly related too while these seniors, outwardly disowned the relationship which this A.S.P. had with them, they wanted the entire matter to be settled to this officer's advantage. But the trouble was that the Sub-Inspector, who launched the complaint, belonged to the caste of the ruling clique. The young S.I. talked of being an old friend of the A.S.P. too and condemned the latter's uppishness. He thought he would have my support, as the political bosses were his caste-men. Nothing of this sort could be done and even the antics of the senior officers surprised me. The case was compromised later, much to the losing of face by the I.P.S. officer. The episode sadly contrasted the stature of the young I.P.S. officer as compared to the I.P. incumbents of old and the equation these officers had with their subordinates. Considering that the A.S.P. was of the first batch of new I.P.S. recruits, the omen appeared to be quite unfavourable. The new I.P.S. had not been able to keep the facade and show their worth as the old officers had done. They could not carry the subordinates with them. The A S.P. had been accused of not attending to his duty and then turning against the subordinate, abusing him in provocative Hindi. The situation as reported was highly unworthy of an officer of the senior service.

A major event of the country were the first general elections. Votes were polled simultaneously for election to the Lok Sabha and State Vidhan Sabha. As this was the biggest ever experiment in adult franchise, very effective police arrangements had to be made, more so as the country was used to the rule of the police force, and nothing could be done unless this force was squarely in the picture. Strictly speaking this was outside the normal sphere of work, but it was claimed that law and order was at stake and required the police to come into the picture. The result was a complete neglect of normal police work culminating in an unprecedented increase in crime during the election period. Also the police became a more positive component of the political scene and were not mere investigators of criminal acts. Law and order keeping had now developed political overtones! This had now been fully entrenched in the system. Rehearsals of police arrangements in the polling booths had to be held now and these were supervised by the State Chief Secretary at some centres in the State capital. He was accompanied not by the Inspector General but by his Deputy, for reasons best known to him. The Chief Secretary had no locus standi in the matter but how else could he be won over to one's side in the game of promotions ? The political tones in the administration were amply evident sometime later when a by-election was held in which the Congress candidate—the Congress had come out with a thumping majority in the elections all over the state—lost to a local adversary. Earlier some special checks were made in this area over payment of sales tax and other government dues and this defeat was ascribed mainly to these checks. The debacle was marked as the Congress had fielded one of their ace candidates and his adversary was only a local small fry. The actual reason for defeat was the Congress candidate's poor image amongst the local populace but this did not seem to register with the high-ups. The result was that the District Magistrate was sent for by the Chief Minister and was given a dressing down for his improper conduct in having made a check for realisation of taxes. So much for polls without political interference. And this continues till today.

As the terrain was difficult, electioneering by the candidates was a tough task. A few days before the general elections the district officer and I were camping in an off-the-track inspection house. We were surprised to find in the morning the local Congress candidate, who was none other than Mrs. Tarkeshwari Sinha, later to become a Deputy Minister in the central government sleeping on the dining table in the rest house. She had had a gruelling day touring on foot from house to house to canvass support. No wonder she won with a thumping majority. The style of operation of the Congress candidates changed quickly and in succeeding elections jeeps and other motor vehicles were used sometimes alienating the voter. During the election period, I covered a lot of ground in a jeep to supervise arrangements. The roads were so dusty that I, who had a sensitive pair of tonsils, donned a gas mask while moving about in the vehicle. This was promptly noticed: this strange policeman doing his rounds with a gas mask inspired considerable fear. To briefly note the arrangements that had been made then: armed police posses were provided at central points and lathi constables at the booths. The armed units did not go into action as the police *izzat* was yet high and a couple of constables, with little education, could keep matters on an even keel. The ballot boxes were collected by armed police parties. The entire work indeed went on like clockwork. But when it came later to dispensing favours like the award of police medals etc., I found that these decorations went only to the officers of the right caste.

During the polls, daily reports had to be prepared of which one copy went to the State Chief Secretary. The typewriter in my office was so old that the carbon copies did not come out well. A few days later the Chief Secretary sent his comments via the I.G.'s office regarding the illegibility of the reports and wanted new machines to be supplied for typing work. The remark amused me as our indents for typewriters had been thrown away with scant consideration: funds were not available in the police department budget. I knew that it was the practice for the reports sent from districts to be kept in some jumble in the secretariat, with nobody bothering to go through these. Some junior assistant, had to prepare a statistical summary for the information of senior officers. The remarks therefore appeared very unusual. No new machines were supplied for several years. The intention was merely to show the personal interest the Chief Secretary took in the affairs of the headquarters district. But that was all. The conditions were so appalling that the police investigating staff did not even have the right quantity of stationery. The records of investigation were generally illegible due to poor carbon paper and were prepared on stationery which was not printed and serially numbered but was purchased locally. How could a junior field officer manage his work without the essential aids? It was known that they would buy their own paper etc., and this came from sources which could not have been approved by departmental regulations. But this did not appear to bother the establishment: as it was considered that these investigators would receive adequate graft money from which these conveniences could be easily found.

During my tenure as S.S.P. Patna, communal trouble cropped up in the sub-divisional town of Biharsharif, later to become headquarters of the newly formed Nalanda District. This sub-divisional town had in its neighbourhood a hillock with the mausoleum of a Muslim *peer*. The story had gone round that this mausoleum was in fact the samadhi of a Hindu mendicant, which has been converted into a grave for the Muslim *peer*. The rioters desecrated the mausoleum by uprooting the pillars which bore some inscriptions from the Quran. When these stone pieces were uprooted and turned round, they were found to contain the symbols of *padma* (lotus) and *sankh* (conch). There was little doubt that this mausoleum had been built up from a Hindu monument. Incensed, the Hindu bigots had attacked a neighbouring

Muslim shrine and a few tenements of the local Muslims were destroyed. Biharsharif with a fairly large Muslim population, had a large majority of Hindus in the area around it. During the British days also several cases of confrontation between the Hindus and the Muslims had taken place. So when we heard of the trouble the incident was unpremeditated—the district officer and myself rushed to the town with police reinforcements and the situtation was promptly brought under control. The indications were however, ominous. The undercurrent of religious jingoism spurred on by pan-Hindu organisations had gathered strength and required to be tackled firmly. In the aftermath of the creation of Pakistan, the feeling was created that Muslims as a whole should migrate there but the new Pakistan would not accommodate them all nor were the Muslims, at least the poorer sections, willing to move there. The agitation was kept simmering however by interested parties. The militant Hindu factions formed the opposite section. The fact that a few pieces of stone from some samadhi had been removed during the long Muslim rule in the country, to build up a mausoleum for a *peer*, could not be used as the reason for perpetration of violence against the Muslims. There was no logic in such an argument and yet incidents like this went on. Having controlled the situations we prompty set up Peace Committees not only in this township but, elsewhere as well so that the violence could be fully contained. There was clear indication of the need for strong controlling forces, but the question was, should these be allied to the local police formations, whose hands were full with their own problems? This matter did not appear to concern anybody—not the government certainly. The picture of the police as the strong arm of the administration maintaining peace at the point of the bayonet, and doing this in preference to police work proper, continued to rule. The incident invited a visit from the Chief Minister of the state, as this sub-division was in the direct charge of his own protege. His visit to the hill top on a palanquin, brought the observation from the common people that the new Indian government was but a replica of the old Nawabhood! All "communal" incidents were the subject of no confidence motions in the state Vidhan Sabha, during which vitriolic speeches were delivered by the Muslim legislators. Even those of the Congress party lent support to this though in a lower key. Such criticism was promptly controlled by distribution of favours to the concerned person. This hardly did justice to the problem that kept it simmering amongst the Muslim intelligentsia.

Casteism and group politics were also slowly gathering momentum in the services and it appeared that in all administrative matters this factor would hold pride of place. There was a function on the eve of the transfer of the District Magistrate of Patna, at the District Congress House. This meeting was attended entirely by Congress workers of the caste (and group) of the incumbent. That a function should be held at the ruling party's office for a government functionary was exceptionable. This was a direct violation of the government servants' conduct rules but it did not appear to trouble the officer concerned or the local Congress. This line up was noticeable in local appointments, which went entirely by the caste of the appointing authority. In the police department it applied to the rank of constable and sub-inspector to which direct recruitment was made locally, in the former case and on local recommendation in the case of the latter. There was a scramble for placing castemen at important points in the police service so as to gain control of the administrative machine. The entire process was a game of chess between caste groups.

During this period, the Prime Minister made a visit to the state headquarters. Arrangements for his security were elaborate but these were being made progressively more rigid. The common practice was to build up barricades to stop the common man from approaching him. This was necessary specially for public meetings, which were arranged as a competitive game between various areas to show how popular he was or how effective the local administration was. The occasion was also utilised for showing off to other local politicians, how much influence the local leader had with the big one and how friendly he was with him. There was an attempt to obtain a seat of vantage in the car which was to carry the Prime Minister and his party and the idea always was to denigrate the State Rajyapal. After all the Rajyapal was usually a politician who had failed in the political game by getting defeated in the elections and had little support inside the party also. The putting up of barricades at railway stations being difficult due to constant movement of trains, the Prime Minister generally arrived by air and travelled about by road. As the Prime Minister wanted the people in general to have his *darshan* from as close quarters as possible, the presence of large crowds was a must. Sometimes the P.M. showed himself to the collected populace by standing in an open car, or on a specially arranged open jeep. However, the position was considerably different when for example the departure or arrival was in the early hours of the morning. How could an audience be collected then ? The P.M. arrived at Patna on the eve of the general elections in 1952 and in connection with the election campaign. He was to depart on a cold wintry morning. We were hard put to arrange a crowd for him. Our efficiency would be fully discounted if a sizable number of people were not at the airport to have his *darshan*. So I arranged to collect the entire lot of constables and their families from the nearby armed police encampment. Nehru was delighted to see the large gathering and talked to them across the barricade. He wished them good cheer. I was apprehensive lest a constable or any member of the family reveal his or her identity. However, delightfully and to my great satisfaction, this contingency did not arise.

There was also a visit by U. Nu, then Prime Minister of the Republic of Burma. He was taken in a motorcade to Nalanda and the hills of Rajgir, then completely undeveloped and full of dusty tracks. U. Nu went in a jeep and knowing his sensitivity to dust, I had arranged gas masks which could be used by him conveniently in certain stretches as I had done during the elections. This pleased him greatly. U. Nu meditated on the hill top at Gridh Kut. We had a difficult time keeping watch over the area as malcontents could get through in the garb of Buddhist monks and could even try to do bodily harm to him. The Ministry of External Affairs officer, who was accompanying him was none other than the daughter of Smt. Sarojini Naidu. She could think of only one enquiry from me, and that was to indicate where the security men were. She had to be told that the policemen in civvies and could not register their presence for obvious reasons. The question amused me greatly. This was indicative of the standard of security, known to the officers of the External Affairs ministry. This newly organised cadre was in urgent need of education in security matters. I was also not happy that all arrangements regarding the visits of VIPs should be made by or through the uniformed police. We had even to provide a baggage officer to look after the personal effects of the high personage. It was time this work was taken over by specialised agencies, leaving the police to perform their duties proper of keeping order on the streets, and bringing law detractors before the bar of justice.

The paradise spot in the country had been ravaged by the marauders from Pakistan soon after partition. Parts of the Jammu and Kashmir State bore the scars of this incursion in a big way when I visited Srinagar and the area around in 1951. The main street in Gulmarg continued to be deserted with shop fronts boarded up after the looting. In this border zone, there was little police activity though some army units were in evidence. The police were surprisingly taking it easy, even in the capital city. The Inspector General of Police of the state was comfortably asleep when I went to call on him about midday. The D.I.G. of C.I.D. was found waiting outside for the boss to shake off the effects of a late night. The I.G. earlier was in the list of precedence a mere Superintendent of Police and officers of this rank were detailed to the state from Indian provinces to act in this capacity. The position was nearly the same now. By contrast, the police in Bihar appeared definitely more up and doing despite the march towards politicisation and sectionalism. This was the level to which police, working on subjective principles, would slide down to. I felt aghast at the prospect and hoped that such a stage would not arise. Succeeding events showed that the portents were quite correct.

The state of discipline in the department, which should have been an example for others to emulate, was well described in the words of an important political worker. His advice was that the boss should be obeyed only if the boss was in the good books of his own boss. Naturally the instances of short-circuiting of authority were numerous. The compliance of orders given was becoming steadily difficult and the number of supervisers required in some cases had to be equal to the number of the workers. While it was considered that at all levels there should be a certain amount of local discretion so that action would fit into the local situation rather than appear to be a parcel of a regimented system, there was no realisation of the stark fact that this discretion was being exercised parochially as the regard for higher authority had well nigh disappeared. A very interesting example was the case in which the fruit grown in the compound of an official's residence were auctioned off on the eve of the season by the temporary incumbent, who was allowed to occupy the accommodation. It was a sizable amount as the compound was fairly large with numerous mango and palm trees. This junior officer pocketed the proceeds with an elan resulting from the fact that he was a member of the minority community and close to the police chief. The new incumbent, a very senior officer, was told that the fruit had been auctioned as they were ripe, and this was permitted by the rules. There was some acrimonious correspondence between the two officers with threats of court action. The sale proceeds should have been shared and the bulk of the amount should have gone to the senior man as the fruit were yet in a very unripe stage, when the change-over had taken place. But no cajoling or argument helped the situation. The fruit in reference—mangoes, became the object of derisive talk in town as all the argument was to decide if the fruit on the trees could be termed as ripe or still in the "baby" stage not fit for plucking. There was another interesting instance in which the wife of a judge of the High Court was involved. She indulged in throwing lavish parties while statutory rationing was on ; she flouted the provisions of the rationing order indicating that meat or fish should not be served by stating quite blandly that what had been served was game, over which there was no control. The chicken served was described as wild fowl and partridge, bagged in a shoot the previous day. But there was no indication that she had gone on any such shoot.

To inculcate courtesy in the police force, I had a set of courtesy slogans prepared in Hindi in the Devnagri script, which were printed on hardboard and were pasted on the walls of all police posts and in particular in the constables' barracks. I made it a routine to call for a recitation of these slogans when I visited police posts. Though ill educated, I felt that the exercise might encourage the constables to learn the Devnagri script and Hindi and also impress on them the importance of courtesy in the performance of their duty. I felt happy that the experience was proving useful when I got a shock on a visit to a police station near Patna, when I enquired of a constable if he knew of the rules of courtesy which had been broadcast to them. Pat came the reply that he had heard of *sujni* bedspread. The Hindi word for courtesy is, *Saujanya.* This word had been cast into a new mould ! I found shortly after I had demitted office in the district that these placards disappeared. These were suffered to exist more to satisfy me and there was no impact at all on the constabulary. Courtesy is still unknown among them. The old incumbents in the police were indeed not amenable to education of any kind and the new incumbents got so mixed up with the old lot that they only followed the pattern already set and had no idea of the work ahead of them. They became little cogs in the machine taking the place of the old worn out pieces.

Rajaji paid a visit to Patna to deliver an address at the local university. He was received at the airport by the Vice-Chancellor Dr. Menon. His wife Mrs. Lakshmi Menon was then a Deputy Minister at the centre. A Minister of the State Government, who also came to receive C.R. introduced the Vice-Chancellor as the husband of Mrs. Lakshmi Menon. This annoyed C.R. who quipped that the Minister himself was better known as his wife's husband. When Rajaji wanted to address the students in the Senate hall, there were demonstrations against him and he was not allowed to speak. I was informed that this had been arranged by this same Minister !

Lord Mountbatten, then Governor General, also came to Patna to preside over a special convocation of the Patna university. The acting V.C. was in the chair. This dignitary, also a Minister in the State Cabinet, had a habit of pronouncing S as Sh. When the time came for investing degrees on the successful students, this acting V.C. would end by saying that "the persons concerned, should by their future behaviour be worthy of the same." The word "same" was pronounced by this person as "shame". The amusement caused near pandemonium in the pandal and Lord Mountbatten had to leave hurriedly. This was followed by another convocation which was attended by Jawaharlal Nehru. The students mobbed him and some pieces of his academic gown—he was to be invested with a doctorate, *Honoris Causa*—were torn away by the disorderly students. On another occasion the State Rajyapal had to retreat by a side road or else he would have been *gherao*-ed and subjected to humiliation : reason, the aimless education policy and neglect of the university campus.

The student community was in a ferment. The members of the state cabinet would not ever make a visit to the university campus for fear of physical obstruction and injury. The police could hardly do anything in the matter, but they were expected to act here also.

The relation between the District Superintendent of Police and the District Magistrate was an established rule in which both functioned as the advisers of each other in achieving objectives, which were identical. This in the past was the maintenance of the Raj.

This system had to go as the common objectives were not clear now– the preservation of national solidarity or democracy had not gone into the people's thinking process. The district officer had to make annual remarks about his brother officer and this was hardly objectionable, as the intention was merely to indicate the strong points of the incumbent rather than indulge in pinpricks. The system now, involving the question of support of boss's boss resulted in these remarks becoming playthings in the hands of inexperienced officers, who did not have the training or even the desire to conform to any standards. Hard work had also lost much of its verve. Earlier the subordinate policeman was expected to be on duty all the time, and he did this under the fear of authority. The senior ranks had a carefree style, as the subordinates were expected to manage the natives effectively. But even though the subordinates did not continue in the same style, the senior ranks continued to do so. On one of the holidays I thought I could utilise my time by doing some inspection work of the police court office—courts were closed on Sundays and holidays and the police staff was available for inspection that day. I was promptly told off by the I.G. for doing this work on a holiday. He considered that the inspection should have been done only on working days ! The atmosphere all round was of letting sleeping dogs lie and to let problems solve themselves in the process of time. The dictum was that the administration would go on, as the day follows the dawn.

The inauguration of the scheme of Community Development in a part of the district was interesting. The idea was little understood. That Community Development Blocks would be spread all over the countryside did not enthuse the people in general who considered that another house of red tape would be added to the many exiting ones. A government office meant harassment to all concerned. This scheme was explained by the Minister in charge of Community Development : he told the villagers that the government had decided to broadcast more money in the countryside under the aegis of this scheme. This was compared to sowing of a crop of paddy or wheat i.e. money would be distributed and like this crop it should multiply. The villagers understood this argument but knew well that the result would be to have another organised misuse of public funds. The scheme of Community Development did not succeed in the country.

We had a visit by film actors and the theatre group fostered by Prithviraj Kapoor of Bombay. Large crowds were drawn specially on occasion of the theatre shows. Prithviraj came with his sons Raj, Shammi, and Shashi: the last two only filled minor roles. Prithviraj would troop out at the end of each show to collect donations and the stampede was a thing to be seen. This theatre group could manage to make both ends meet with such donations. The process was reminiscent of the days when Mahatma Gandhi would spread out sheets of cloth at the end of his meetings for assistance to the Harijans. However, the premieres of some of the films, presented serious problems. The well known actress of the time, Kamini Kaushal was on a visit on the occasion of the premiere show of one of the films in which she had played the title role. The news of her coming was properly advertised. Result : the car in which she travelled to the cinema hall was surrounded by her fans. A piece of the sari she was wearing was torn off by her admirers as a memento. This happened in spite of all police arrangements. The public were in no mood to be restrained from frivolity. Kamini Kaushal promptly withdrew from the scene, and this led to the cinema screen being torn up by the crowd. Soon after independence, the people in general had started the game of flouting the police, whose regulating process they had always detested, little appreciation that the crux of the problem was, what was to be enforced. Here the police were trying to arrange things so that all concerned could enjoy the show but the people hardly appreciated this. This resulted in most functions ending in a fiasco. The police became increasingly ineffective.

In the administrative system, it was the trifles which mattered. A little slip in paying respect to a political personage or a checking made of a member of the legislature, while going into the hall where the legislature met, would cause considerable furore. A good part of the time of the legislature would be taken up in discussing such matters. The police were not taken off the duty posts in the legislatures; the institution of the Marshal had yet to come. There was also no analysis of the working of the police department or for that matter of any other department. Matters of import like planning were left to stipendiary officers revelling in playing to the tune of their bosses, when the latter hardly knew anything about it all. The economic situation in particular was getting out of hand. It was assuming the shape of things in neighbouring China, where Chiangkai Shek's administration had to face a complete rout at the hands of the new revolutionaries. So far as the police in the country was concerned, the trend was to make appropriate placing of senior personnel who could anticipate the wishes of the bosses. Legal or constitutional provisions did not matter. The effect was to subjectivise all work. Ministers would take no notice of officers, who they themselves desired should remain present at the airport or railway station or even the rest house (in case of a road journey), at the time of their arrival. This made them feel doubly important. The senior officers waited patiently for the VIP's attention and this was possible with the assistance of the security men who surrounded the VIP. These aides showed regard for the senior police officers, as they knew, they could be repatriated to their original job in the department under the bosses, who required their assistance now. The officers who did not keep these rules of hanging round were relegated to the back bench and public disapproval was often heaped on them by the leaders. A junior A.S.P., who was later to become the chief of the C.B.I., told me of his plight ; he had been denigrated for no fault of his in a public meeting in Sasaram, a small sub-divisional town.

It was a moot point who should take the salute on the occasion of formal parades at the State headquarters. The problem kept haunting the scene and no solution was possible. The Rajyapal had been denigrated greatly and the Chief Minister, therefore, took the line convenient to himself so that there may not be any loss of face for the head of the State as well. If the Rajyapal was available at the State headquarters the Chief Minister would conveniently move away to the summer headquarters of the government at Ranchi. But it had to be ensured that the various formalities connected with the functions both at Patna and Ranchi were the same. This provided good fun to many and later resulted in a prolonged debate in the press if the Rajyapal was really needed in new situation. These debates continue even now, though intermittantly.

I tried to introduce new methods of control particularly in investigation of serious offences. But I received several setbacks. There was a big sensation in the city on the news of an entire family in the low income group being wiped out. The house was looted, but the amount involved could not have been more than a few hundred rupees. It was a clear case of vendetta as no factor of sex was involved. By careful analysis of the fingerprints which were found at the spot, the entire mystery was unravelled by the senior investigators but it took quite some time to do so. The result was a public disapproval of the police functioning. There was also a case in which the Mahant of a religious Math mounted an attack on a neighbouring Math. He misguided the primary police investigator and this was rendered possible as he had the support of certain important persons in the area. The scientific examination of bullet marks on the door frame conducted by a senior officer gave the lie to the story. The case was worked out but it also took some time. Apparently public expectancy of police efficiency was going up while the working methods were not improving in the same proportion. This hiatus had worried me considerably and it was in this context that I had prepared a scale for investigation of cases indicating the involvement of senior officers. This system was not liked by the senior officers as they wanted to ride on the tribulations of their subordinates and the law indicated that the primary investigator was entirely responsible. No change in this system could be brought about by me even though I had made a good experiment.

The standard of assistance that I could obtain could be gauged from the behaviour of a senior officer who was posted as Superintendent of Police in the city. He was placed in charge of police arrangements on the occasion of the Republic Day celebrations. Rather than prepare a chart of postings he left the matter to his subordinates and when asked how he was going to deploy the available force, he came out with the astounding order to the constables that they should go and take their posts as in the past as such observances and functions were quite frequent. He was questioned by the State Chief Minister in an earlier charge, why crimes had registered an increase even though this officer had the reputation of being a "crime controller". His reply was that the number of Ministers had also registered an unprecedented increase, so why not crimes as well. Being of a caste-group opposed to that of the Chief Minister, no action was taken as it would have been misconstrued in the political circles as vendetta against the other group. Another officer, who belonged to the Brahmin fraternity, had his own ways. He toured about in an old Ford car when on his rounds at night, he would repeat *Hanuman Chalisa* (a prayer) that kept the car going and also according to him, kept the criminals at bay !

I now got a move to the Government of India in the Ministry of Home Affairs. I had had a full tenure at Patna for three years and normally also I would have been moved. I was extremely happy to get this transfer. But the press came out with glowing editorials about my tenure in Patna and I was frightened that this arrangement may be upset. Luckily this did not happen.

8

GOVERNMENT OF INDIA

THE INDIAN POLICE cadres in the country were so framed as to provide incumbents for the "police" jobs in the Government of India. The number of these jobs was indeed very small and there was therefore no need for the maintenance of a central police pool as was appropriate for the Indian Civil Service. Selection for a post in the Government of India was considered in many ways a lift as it involved a sizeable amount of special pay. There was also little scope for advancement in the States. But in view of State-autonomy, this posting could also imply that perhaps those who were sent out could not fit into the local grooves either because of their lack of accord with state orchestration or their inability to stand up to the politics which had become the hallmark of administration in each State.

The ministries in the Government of India, functioned as mini-empires. The general impression was of the Chief Minister acting as a local potentate while the Central Ministers were hemmed in by the Prime Minister, who was often likened to a democratic dictator. The State Chief Ministers also followed the pattern adopted by the Prime Minister and it became the style for them even to carry a swagger cane, as was done by the Prime Minister. The office decor was similarly copied : was not imitation the best form of flattery ? There were some attempts at horse-riding and yoga, for which Jawaharlal Nehru was quite famous. In the central government with its wide expanse, each functionary, big or small, felt like a mini cog in a giant machine. Even the ministers had a similar feeling as they had to wait endlessly to obtain an audience with the Prime Minister. In this milieu, the fact that the Intelligence set-up had an easy access to the Prime Minister was an item of considerable jealousy. Even those in the political circles, envied this privilege. The Intelligence officers drawn from the police, had thus a special position. But that was all as in the field whether in the States or in the Union Territory, the police continued to function as the underdog.

The entire police set-up in the capital was under the care of a Superintendent of Police, who was indeed so low-down in the hierarchy that he hardly mattered. There was no other prestigious police set-up at the centre and there were only a couple of officers of the rank of Inspector General. Thanks to Parkinson's law, the number of I.Gs has increased nearly twenty fold within about two decades. There are now a plethora of police organisations rubbing shoulders with each other and even having overlapping functions.

In the Home Ministry there were interesting interludes. Officers were posted here but they had no place to sit and carry on the duties of their office. The lucky ones were provided a seat, but inkpots, paper, and the usual claptrap of office took a long time to be supplied. The Superintendent of one of the sections working under me, had the temerity to telephone the Superintendent of the Establishment section and talking in Bengali told him that the newly posted officers appeared to be in a hurry and they wanted the office equipment to be provided without delay. How was this possible ? Great was his discomfiture when he found that his lingo was understood by me fully.

When I joined at Delhi, Dr. Kailash Nath Katju was the Home Minister. He was later to become the Chief Minister of Madhya Pradesh. He was forgetful by nature though well-meaning. During his chief ministership, he visited Raipur and was met by a local deputation headed by a Deputy Minister of the State. During the interview Katju Saheb stated that it was coincidental that he had a Deputy Minister in his own cabinet of the same name as that of the leader of this delegation. The junior minister felt much perturbed over the lack of recognition by his leader. Later Pt. Govind Ballabh Pant became the Home Minister. It was said about him that he read files while in the bath !

The country was agog with the news about the budget leakage. This led ultimately to the resignation of the Finance Minister, Shanmukham Chetty. The leakages were known to have occurred during the process of printing. All this was investigated by officers of the I.B. and the government officials responsible were tracked down and dealt with according to law. Nothing specific could be found against Chetty. However, a State Minister in Vindhya Pradesh was trapped about this time while accepting graft money. A Bihar cadre police officer who was presiding over the department of police in the state (a C-Class state) wittily described it as *Vichitra Pradesh*. The Home Minister of this state had ways all his own of dealing with matters in his purview. He was known to have ordered the detention of a public transport at the police station as the operator did not conform to his orders for giving a free ride to his friends. His forte was to demand abject submission to official directions. But for all anti-corruption work, the only agency at the central level was the Special Police establishment, and it dealt with the doings mainly of stipendiary staff in the central sphere, and marginally in the state spheres. The ministers went scot-free, unless the P.M. took a personal interest in the matter and put some one specially on the job like the one in Vindhya Pradesh. At the centre a minister was reported to have had some shady involvement in Nepal but nothing happened : he even had the image of being a very honest politician.

The state of administration in the central secretariat was a little better than that in vogue in the states. One of the departmental secretaries, now termed as secretary to the ministry, boasted at a dinner that it was easy for him to carry on his duties as he could bring the minister and the deputy at loggerheads. The two wrangling ministers enabled the secretary to rule the roost. This secretary did not have too high a reputation for integrity and his philandering escapades were only too well known. Some other senior civil servants were known to be maintaining expensive apartments in local hotels where call-girls could be invited. I had the mortification of seeing the manner of functioning of a senior officer who lived next-door to me. This flat was the rendezvous of young girls of various nationalities. This however, did not seem to affect their careers. The police should function as the keepers of the morals of the administrative ranks and should be able to control violations of the established law. This role the police in the country was not capable of performing. On the other hand the fact that intelligence was strong with police echelons was making both ineffective and may perhaps have ushered in Gestapo to cover the country.

The democratisation of the country's Constitution did not usher in an era of socialising the in-service behaviour of the public servant. An officer one rank above had to be pompously addressed as "Sir". The normal correspondence was previously suffixed as "I have the honour to be sir, your most obedient servant". This was replaced by two simple words "Yours faithfully". I was mortified, however, to see the compendious instructions indicating which officer should be addressed as "Dear so and so", or "My dear so and so" or even "Dear Mr. so and so". All this went with the rank of the writer and the person to whom the letter was addressed. *Esprit de corps* which was the hallmark of the police service, and should in fact be the characteristic of any service, had now degenerated and jobs stratified at various levels. It was now not customary for a senior officer to call on another officer who may be even one place junior to him and occupying a slightly smaller position. In the sphere of general report writing, it was a surprise to find the reports of junior officers being rehashed to appear as pieces emanating from the superior officers themselves. There was a distinct tone of subjectivism and, objective reporting which was the need of the hour, was not to be found. In the absence of expertise among senior politicians the administration had to be led by bureaucrats. But the bureaucrats had placed faith in the dictum of making hay while the sun shines. An intelligence officer, whom I happened to meet frequently, was known to have connections with the high-ups and this carried him a long way. He could hardly write any report but continued to earn promotions. His connections did the trick, which hard work and ability could not have achieved.

I was travelling by train in a four-berth first class compartment from Patna to Delhi. Although I had my berth reserved, I was mortified to find it occupied by a *khaddar* clad pontiff. It was a job to get the place vacated with the intercession of the railway staff. Some police officers in uniform were there to see me off. This appeared to be not to the liking of this dignitary. I forgot about the incident, but about a month later I received a note from the Home Minister virtually calling for my explanation—the person concerned was an M.P. and he had stated that the behaviour of the police officials in reference was very rude. He had not stated that the railway officials had a job making the M.P. vacate the berth that he had occupied unauthorisedly. I was very unhappy at all this particularly when I had been a silent spectator of the happenings in the railway compartment.

I had to contend with the problem of India's northern and north eastern frontier while in Delhi. A scheme prepared to put the entire set up under one channel of control with an officer of the rank of Deputy I.G. Police in charge was received coldly, yet not long after a huge organisation, para-military in character, was set up. An argeement on Trade and Transit in the Tibet region of China was finalised and I had a share in the goings on. It appeared that there was little appreciation of the danger posed by China on this front. A few wireless stations were set up in these areas but it was difficult to obtain even minor items for them leave aside the technical equipment. Those available were at best rudimentary. In connection with this work I visited the northern sector of the country on the Tibetan (Chinese) border. Returning by train from one of these visits, I had to travel by a Janata train through parts of North Bihar. I kept my towel, soap etc. in the bathroom attached to the compartment but discovered a little later that they were missing. As the compartment was not crowded, my gunman inquired among the passengers about the articles and requested that the items be returned, if they had been taken by mistake. Subsequently, the passengers agreed to have their persons searched. The towel was located tied to the person of one of the men and the other things were also concealed by him. Rather than agree to handing over the miscreant to the police at the next halt, the passengers attempted to deal with him stating that train robberies had become rather frequent in that section. It was indeed a job to desist them and the culprit in any case was not penitent as it appeared that he was a habitual offender in the line. Travel by train was extremely hazardous and pickpocketing and snatching were the order of the day. The erstwhile Railway Protection Force, which I had headed, had been disbanded and instead guarding of rail property became the responsibility of a special force attached to the railway administration. They were armed to provide protection to railway property against marauders but the safety of the travelling public was the job of the Railway Police which continued to be attached to the state police formations. And indeed these had become entirely inefficient and had the reputation of being hand in glove with thieves and robbers whose depredations they had to stave off. Even the railway administration would get announcements made at all halts calling on the passengers to be careful—that was the protection given. The Railway police believed in palming off responsibility as incidents when reported, were alleged to have occurred elsewhere and the papers went from post to post unattended, affording no relief to the victims of these perfidious acts. The Government of India appointed the Director of the Intelligence Bureau to examine the question of security services on the railways, which meant merely looking at the losses incurred by the railway administration in the process. Obviously this was a very limited approach, more so as the job was entrusted to one who could hardly have done justice to it. The police work on the railways is in the doldrums even now and no bold steps have been proposed or effected.

During the stay in Delhi, I was witness to the welcome accorded to the Russian duo Bulganin and Khrushchev. In the metropolis, school children were mobilized to make this function tumultuous. Even the officials working in the North and South Blocks, lined the route in front of their offices to have a view of the *tamasha*.

The police arrangements all through were very elaborate, resulting in caustic comments about the popularity of the visitors and even the national leadership at home. The populace showed little discipline and the capacity of the establishment in stage managing shows appeared extremely limited.

On the occasion of the first air power display arranged near Delhi at Tilpat, about this time, the movement of traffic was jammed for nearly twenty four hours. A majority of the people were not able to reach Tilpat at all. The Prime Minister arrived by helicopter to find a large part of the gallery vacant. He naturally took to task the local administration and a full dress enquiry was ordered into the lapses of the traffic police. It was clear that the police generally and in particular the traffic police were quite incapable of handling a show like this, nor were the road conditions suited to such heavy traffic. Living on the Wellesley Road in the newly built government flats, I had also intended to go to Tilpat but was lucky to be back from near Okhla by midday. The bombing demonstration caused a severe rattle in the window panes in my flat so far from Tilpat. It was reassuring that the air force was using effective missiles, such as were available internationally then.

The rehearsals for the 26th January celebrations were being polished up and though in the early phase, the show itself was enjoyed by one and all. The police bandobast was satisfactory and devices like walkie-talkie sets were used for communication. But the pace of progress seems to have been retarded making the police in Delhi one of the most backward echelons of any city of the world. At that time Delhi had a rural look with no high rise buildings. The population was less than a million. The entire city police work was managed with half a dozen police stations as the south Delhi area had not developed at all. Therefore the set-up was perhaps good enough to carry on but progress shall have been made as development took place. Apparently even important matters were handled unimaginatively.

The Chief Minister of Bihar was on a visit to the capital. Such visits were not too frequent then ; now the C.Ms spend most of their time in Delhi. In several cases full fledged establishments are maintained at State expense during their stay in the capital. In fact each State has developed a Bhawan in Delhi in addition with a liaison officer of the rank of Commissioner to look after its maintenance. These officers are jocularly designated as the State-ambassadors accredited to the Delhi Darbar. To revert, the Chief Minister of Bihar was staying with a Deputy Minister of the Central government. I was surprised to find the Revenue Minister of Bihar, later to become the Chief Minister of Bihar—walking up and down the lawns of the house. When I went to call on the C.M. I was told by the Minister that he was waiting for the *Malik* to get ready. This was the typical style of working of the Zamindari estates in Bihar wherein the Divan, the chief manager, was to act as the master's major domo. Usually the Divan was a Kayastha while the Zamindar was a Bhumihar, a Rajput, or a Muslim Nawab who had lost his ruling powers and had become a mere zamindar. Here the Kayastha Revenue Minister was waiting on the Bhumihar Chief Minister ! The same day the Chief Minister met the officers from Bihar, who were attached to various ministries, and requested them to help the state ! The entire system appeared to be retrograde and tickled me greatly. One of the officers recommended to the C.M. not to trust the police officers from the State turned intelligence officers at the Centre. This was too absurd for words and the C.M. also had a long laugh at the suggestion.

K.S.V. Raman, a senior I.C.S. officer from Bihar, was on a visit to Delhi and went into the South Block to call on the Foreign Secretary, his compeer in the service. He moved up and down the corridor meeting some friends and finally barged in on the Personal

Assistant of the Foreign Secretary to be told that the officer was not available for interview. Undeterred Raman made another round of the corridor and this time forced himself into the Foreign Secretary's room. He was surprised to find his friend busy with his files though the indication outside was "engaged". Raman informed this officer that a little while earlier he had called in and was told that the Saheb was not available. But the Foreign Secretary informed him that he was all the time in the room and could scarcely take the risk of foraying out, lest he find the seat occupied by another incumbent when he returned !

An annual conference of Deputy Inspectors General of Police of States in charge of the C.I.D., which included both the crime and the intelligence wings, was held under the aegis of the Home Ministry. This meant that the entire organisation and minuting work as also the follow-up action had to be done by the Intelligence Bureau. Once in two years, the State Inspectors General met and this job was also the responsibility of the I.B. Being the prime intelligence agency of the country, the I.B. found it easier to settle matters with the comparatively junior functionaries of the intelligence department of the police attending the D.I.Gs' conference but with the I.Gs, it was an uphill task. The Director of the Intelligence Bureau was by no standards the seniormost nor even the most competent of the lot of Inspectors General. Some of the senior I.Gs were very critical of what was happening and the Director, who was to preside over these meetings, was hard put to keep order. The Director I.B. was initially equivalent in rank to an I.G. Police and therefore the job was no attraction to any State police chief. Later this was slightly upgraded : even this did not attract adequate respect from the I.Gs in the country. The state I.G. still wielded considerable power and prestige which the Director I.B. did not. Police being a state subject, the conference of the state police chiefs was just a ritual and nothing substantial was expected to be achieved. Perhaps a little fraternisation of the police chiefs was all that could be done, but if taken seriously the forum could work as the jumping board of reforms. Even with the D.I.Gs. the aspect of crime found the Bureau hesitating as hardly any infrastructure existed at the Centre to coordinate matters. The S.P.E. which dealt with corruption, did not fulfil this role and the Central Bureau of Investigation laid on in the country's Constitution, had yet to materialise.

The most interesting part of the two exercises mentioned above was the address by the Home Minister and the Prime Minister, Jawaharlal Nehru in his rambling addresses talked in general terms of India's foreign policy and ended up with an exhortation to the police officers to mend their fences. That was about all and left us generally highly dissatisfied. He would sometimes set down to asking questions like when he was arrested in the NWFP etc. He naturally expected that intelligence officers would have the answers on their finger tips, he was sadly disillusioned. As he continued with his address Jawaharlal would carry on his chain smoking which somehow did not fit into the general picture we had of a public leader. The P.M's personal security was the responsibility of the I.B. and through them of the State police formations. This was one point on which the I.B. talked with authority as the entire country was functioning as a political monolith with the Congress party at the head under the undisputed leadership of Nehru. All the security arrangements had the approval of Nehru. The Home Minister Pt. Kailash Nath Katju was busy in effecting some change in the Code of Criminal Procedure. He would exhort the police chiefs to resign from their posts if any person in a police lock up died an unnatural death. This was hardly practical. Even the reforms in the Criminal Procedure Code, in which Katju showed much interest, merely scratched the surface. The maladies were deep rooted and appeared not to attract attention. Pt. Pant who followed Dr. Katju, made an impression but his physical infirmity militated against his being a successful Home Minister. He waxed eloquent about regional problems and set going the zonal councils. But the follow-up was fitful and therefore ineffective.

There was a great deal of talk and very little was achieved. In the sectional meetings which were held, for example, in the S.P.E., the main item was to boost the ego of even the Joint Secretary in the Ministry who dealt with the subject. International technical conferences regarding crime and general intelligence were attended by junior functionaries of the Ministry in addition to I.B. officers and some state police chiefs. Obviously the idea was to enable these officers of the ministry to have a jaunt abroad and thus keep them on the right side for getting schemes approved by the Ministry.

The I.B. sported an intercommunication system for use in office. This contraption was employed in almost all industrial and commercial houses, and the railways in a big way. I was told that there was regular eavesdropping on the newly acquired officers, perhaps as a security check. The inter-communication system was later given up as the security check disclosed that the officers of the I.B. mainly specialised in *Kamasutra* and the *Playboy* brand of stories ! One of the officers was always worried about the crease of his trousers and was busy wiping his face with a perfumed handkerchief. Another officer was so proud of his style of expression in the English language that he would waste the entire time crossing the 't's and dotting the 'i's in drafts. The objective should have been to produce an understandable and clear report and not to emulate R.L. Stevenson or G.B. Shaw !

Nehru was anxious to rid the administrative machine of the mass of chaprassis and hangers on. In the Central Secretariat, the corridors were full of these functionaries lounging around and yet the Ministers would not move out without the entourage of chaprassis and their seniors, Daffadars or Jamadars. This exercise was a complete failure and it only stiffened the attitude of the grade IV employees towards their duties. There was no improvement in their efficiency, which alone could result in reduction of their numbers. The chaprassis would not even perform their normal work. When they arrived in the morning, they first had the drying-time when they got over the sweat and grime of the journey from their residence to the office. Then followed an exchanging notes session and the inevitable cup of tea. A short spell of work was succeeded by a lunch interval, after which they were all in a mood to doze ; followed by tea and a long preparatory session for quitting. The plea for going earlier was the lack of accommodation in buses. Even the question of phasing the work hours was examined but was given up. The same routine applied to the assistants. The officers, however, stayed for long hours but many preferred to leave the car till late hours in the line of the head of department's car while they walked back home. Obviously the boss was expected to feel that the junior incumbents were at the job for long and late hours.

In regard to his own security (and which vicariously applied to the President as well) Jawaharlal allowed himself to be led up the garden path, being told that in view of some threatening letters received and the earlier assassination of Mahatma Gandhi, he should have a tight cordon round him. All this meant that he was removed from contact with people, whose favourite he was reported to be. In fact it was customary to send out an officer of the rank of S.P. (or even a D.I.G.) to go out with him for ensuring his security in the visits to the states, where the details had to be worked out by the local police and intelligence agencies. These arrangements appeared to be a replica of what applied to the Head of State in the U.K. while touring in the colonies, when these were administered by the Britishers. This was hardly appropriate now. Yet the arrangements were made more and more rigid with the march of time and now an officer of the rank of Inspector General goes along with the P.M. for checking the arrangements in a job that could possibly be done by a much smaller man. The barricades which were put up cost a fortune and caused caustic comments in public forums.

During my years in the Ministry of Home Affairs I found that government had no personnel policy worth the name, specially in the I.B. to which I was attached. I had come with promise of promotion but was unhappy to find that my compeers in the State were going forward, while at the central level, we were stuck in our seats. It appeared that one could earn promotion here if there was a political pull as promotions were distributed as favours to cronies, and near and dear ones. The Persian adage—*Murrabi beyaar murabba bakhor*—have a good life if you have a patron—could not be apter. This was a depressing situation. However the result was repatriation to the State cadre to earn normal promotion.

9

BIHAR RUMBLES

I WAS back in the State cadre in good time to celebrate the first decade of independence and also to take a hand in the second general elections. During this period, there was no improvement in the working of the police : If anything there was a slight backward march with graft coming to the fore. The prevalent corruption was reminiscent of the Mughal darbar, where graft was the order of the day and was in fact considered a *mamul* i.e. a matter of routine. Corruption had led to large scale nepotism. Whereas in the pre-independence period there was hardly any question of doubting the bonafides particularly of the top echelons, it appeared that they now set the pattern in corruption and nepotism. Earlier, senior officers were told about their impending transfers and arrangements in the chain of senior officers proceeding on leave were made in good time. The establishment method was to let a junior officer continue to officiate in a higher rank by the seniors taking leave by turns. Now it was the fashion for officers not to proceed on leave and they trotted out the story that they were indispensable. This assertion was perhaps actuated by the fact that leave might mean a change of post and attendant complications regarding schooling of children etc. In the pre-independence period, the officer coming from England arranged the schooling and higher education of his children at Home and therefore a change in posting did not affect him. These officers were bothered only when their turn for promotion became due and transfer was necessary. The picture was, however, different with Indian incumbents. The political powers also found the game of posting interesting and profitable. Therefore, the entire system of these promotions and postings, as was known earlier, required change so that it may be fruitful. It was time a system of compulsory leave was introduced as old officers in feeble health continued at their posts of duty, adding to the atmosphere of inefficiency. On each question the views of the people who mattered were so different that the picture was indeed of the tower of Babel, each man voicing and acting according to his own likes.

On repatriation to the State from the Home Ministry, I was placed in charge of several D.I.G. level jobs till I was firmly fixed as Range D.I.G. at Ranchi, with jurisdiction over the entire Chhota Nagpur Division. I worked in the Special Branch of the C.I.D. for a brief period and was witness to the gerrymandering that went on over the selection of candidates by the principal political parties and later in the management of the election campaign. The Special Branch was the single intelligence organisation of the State and was tagged to the police department. To fulfil their targets, this department had to employ informants of various sorts and for that the available funds were kept beyond the purview of audit. The amount was not large and the results achieved earlier were a clear pointer to the system. With the schism in the ruling group, the Special Branch was confused about who their agents should be, specially as they were required to feed the Chief Minister with the happenings and goings on in the opposing faction in his own party also. A little later coalitions came on and the job amounted to seeking intelligence about one party in the government with the hope of helping the other. It was indeed an uphill task and some indications of it were available even now. The question of personal loyalties of the officers of the Special Branch, therefore, came up.

In regard to final allocations for secret work, the grants mounted several fold, with no visible results. Each Minister had a small discretionary grant at his disposal but it irked him that while proper accounting and audit procedures applied to these sums, the case of the Special Branch funds was different. A fraction of the discretionary funds expenditure, where the rules would not appear to be fully satisfied, was therefore channelled through this branch. The S.B. had to satisfy a variety of demands on this fund from other higher quarters as well. Carpets and electrical gadgets including cameras, dictaphones etc. would now have to be supplied to some officers for use even at residences. The more difficult job was to dole out funds to officers of the police who had to render accounts to the departmental head. Senior officers wanted a slice without proferring any account, and the S.B. head, sometimes junior to these officers, found it difficult to evade this for fear he getting into trouble with these officers. In this process, intelligence work was the first casualty. The subordinates also pandered to those who would be helpful to them and the political bosses thought they could utilise them for their personal advantage. The Chief of the S.B. had to be a pliant tool in the hands of the concerned politicians, and with an easy conscience if he wished to get on. Effective work was no yardstick of his efficiency. His continuance in this coveted post was like tight rope walking and he could have adequate financial gain and political patronage in the bargain. The job was entirely unenviable.

In the general elections that took place in 1957, the Congress party returned to power in Bihar though with a slightly decimated majority. The position was the same in other states. The election of a party leader for the State Legislature was an acrimonious contest between the two warring groups. And when the result of the contest was announced, there was a victory march on behalf of the winning party with slogans that were decidedly provocative. The police had to perform the task of preventing the two factions of the ruling party coming to grips. In particular the C.I.D. were expected to know who would win and perhaps exert their influence in the matter. As the group in power was returned again, the police and the C.I.D. remained largely intact. As I was in the S.B. the winning group had somehow mistakenly expected that I would provide intelligence to them of the goings on in the other group. I clearly indicated that this was not in the C.I.D.'s charter and I could do little about it. If I had taken sides, I would no doubt have had favours bestowed on me, the thesis being : "not with us, then against us". I knew I would now be pushed out of the S.B. This in fact took place and I was posted to distant Ranchi. The Chief Minister was reported to have said that I was a great disappointment and that I belonged to the other caste-group ! Another important aspect was that both the intelligence organisations of the Central and the State governments worked entirely independently, although they drew their staff from the police department of the State. These intelligence wings very often acted at cross purposes, each suspecting the other of some diabolical plans. Their reports were now generally coloured and not entirely reliable ! It was time this confused state was sorted out but this had no place in the list of priorities. A positive personnel policy was required and also if two parallel agencies for collection of internal intelligence were really necessary.

The administrative looseness and the emphasis on wrong ponits had resulted in the entire disciplinary fabric getting askew. The confusion in transfers, postings, and promotions as indicated earlier had resulted in laxity of local functions. There followed a further sharp increase in crime generally. In particular, dacoities—a form of mediaeval crime characterised by use of force by organised groups—multiplied several fold. The attempt of the police investigators in the middle and subordinate ranks, was to paint not too bleak a picture and this could be done by not recording cases or by minimising their gravity and seriousness. The officers were anxious to jockey for positions and play soft with certain sections even though these were criminally inclined where they should have been strong and impartial. The criminals therefore had little to fear from the police. Earlier, it was the common talk that crimes and the criminals associated with them were known to the police but they brought to book only those who were considered inconvenient for their operations. Now the picture was one of a police force with no contacts at the grass-roots level and completely ignorant of who were the likely perpetrators of these crimes. There were other areas of ineptitude also. While the strength of the armed police and the quality of their arms went up, there was no sign of adoption of new training techniques and improvement in recruitment standards. The new personnel was therefore not effective. The expectations of the people were much higher, which this demoralised and inappropriate force could not achieve.

The Chief Secretary, an officer of the I.C.S. belonged to the State but had developed strong links with neighbouring U.P. where he had had his education at Allahabad university. This university had the reputation of having produced a galaxy of seasoned administrators, scientists and teachers. It had therefore become the fashion in Bihar for young men to join that university for their education. This officer was commonly understood as a supporter of the Bhumihars though himself a Rajput. As Cabinet Secretary he could in more ways than one aid in moulding government policy. Though apparently firmly in position, he was suddenly transferred after the 1957 elections as a Joint Secretary in the Union Home Ministry. This was obviously the resultant of caste intrigue. The transfer incensed the Rajput group in Bihar both in the government and outside and it was clear that caste politics was going to have a stranglehold in the affairs of the State in a really big way now. The departure of this officer by train, caused some interest as the Chief Minister was at the station to see him off. He travelled with him in the train up to Arrah, headquarters of the district of Shahabad. The local press indicated this as the double face of politicians, but it was disclosed later that the Chief Minister had actually proceeded then to spend some time with a junior police officer, who had married the daughter of a very close friend of his.

The Range to which I was transferred was co-terminus with the revenue division, which comprised the entire hilly terrain in south Bihar with large industries and rich minerals. It had a large scheduled tribe population, poor in health and economically very backward. The officer from whom I had to take over charge was due to retire on relief. He had consulted a palmist and astrologer who was close to the C.M., and had been informed by him that he would continue to be in office for a further term of a year or so. However, to his great disappointment this prophecy did not come true. The merriment to the subordinates was obvious.

On arrival at Ranchi, I was accommodated for some time in the local forest department rest house, as my predecessor had not vacated the official residence. This bungalow did not have a phone connection. I would have found it difficult to manage the affairs of my charge without this convenience. I was therefore agreeably surprised to find a temporary telephone line extended to my room even without my asking for it. Later the local telephone chief came to call on me, from whom I learnt that a case had been instituted against him some time back in which his house-maid alleged that he had attempted to outrage her modesty. The case was pending police investigation. It was clear why the P & T staff were so prompt in providing me with a telephone. Pending the investigation, police officers had found that they got a favourable treatment at the hands of the telephone department incumbents! Therefore they dragged their feet. I saw to it that the police investigation was completed with due alacrity. Even though the police found no evidence worth the name to substantiate the charge, the matter was raked up and was taken to court. The telephone engineer was ultimately honourably acquitted. All this indeed gave a very poor image to the police. I sought to change this by improving public relations and ensuring quick disposal of investigation of cases. This was merely a prick on the deep distrust against the police which had developed over decades. I knew that I could not do much in this direction in the prevailing climate.

I found a considerable movement of officers of all ranks in their areas ostensibly for public work. My predecessor had informed me that he had made an analysis of which the conclusion was that no touring was undertaken by any officer for his normal duties and these were entirely arranged for personal reasons viz., sightseeing, meeting friends or establishing contacts. This was the reason why postings had assumed great importance. The officers wanted to be posted at convenient places from where they could look after their personal affairs at the cost of the State exchequer. The expenditure on travelling allowance had multiplied ten fold during ten years of independence and no amount of government circulars could curb the tendency as the law-makers were the first to violate the rules. A standard question raised in the Vidhan Sabha related to the amount of travelling allowance drawn by ministers. The figures indicated that usually this allowance far exceeded the pay packet and it had the advantage of being income tax free. The rates of travelling allowance allowed to these members of government were very liberal—a car was provided at government cost along with a chauffeur and only for the gas put into it, the approved allowance was a rupee a mile.

The industrial belt in south Bihar held the important TISCO Works at Jamshedpur, also known as Tata Nagar. A large number of private sector units were also located here, engaged in the manufacture of various items connected with the locally produced steel. Jamshedji Tata had established India's first steel mill in the face of considerable official apathy, and had succeeded in setting up a very sound unit, with a contended labour force, which was looked after well. Tata Iron and Steel Works along with the Indian Iron and Steel Works near Asansol and the small Bhadrawati Works in the south, constituted the entire steel production in the country, all in the private sector. There was labour trouble in TISCO mills, however, in 1958 partly engineered by the Communist party, who were attempting to get a hold over the labour union, so far led by Michael John, a pro-Congress Indian National Trade Union Congress leader. There was some trouble during the last nearly a decade but the law and order machinery of the state had continued to be archaic with no control room even to boast of.

The affairs of the police were overseen by an Additional Superintendent of Police, working in a wing of the local sub-divisional officer's office. During the agitation in 1958 therefore it was a job to act effectively. A shanty market was set on fire by criminal elements. When the Deputy Commissioner came from the neighbouring township of Chaibasa, which was his headquarters, and along with the Additional Superintendent of Police and his men faced the riotous group of the Communist labour union, he was hit with a shower of stones. He had to order firing in which quite a few lives were lost. The Army units had to be called out too. The Army Commander located at Lucknow rushed to Jamshedpur. Matters were brought under control with me fixed at Jamshedpur for a considerable period of time and the agitators were placed behind bars, but my despair was the low morale of the police. When firing had to be resorted to, it was found that almost all the armed constables had made themselves scarce. Only three or four constables who could be held together physically by the additional S.P. ultimately carried out the orders of firing.

After order had been restored, Tatas arranged the opening of a park in Jamshedpur christened the Jubilee Park as it coincided with the golden jubilee of the founding of the factory. Appropriately this park was inaugurated by Prime Minister Jawaharlal Nehru. Considerable propaganda was made by the Communist as the Prime Minister stayed during the visit in the Director's bungalow of the TISCO. This was considered to symbolise the capitalist bias of the country's government. The labour trouble in TISCO earlier had affected the production of steel and impinged on other industries in the country in more ways than one. A proposal was then made by the leftists that this factory should be nationalised. But efforts were also afoot to set up steel mills in the public sector and not long after units at Durgapur, Rourkela, and Bhilai and later at Bokaro in the Chhota Nagpur belt of Bihar came up. The TISCO steel mill is still in the private sector. The TISCO unit was nationalised as also the Bhadravati Works. TISCO continues to do well while not all the public sector projects appear to be doing as well.

The Army Commander, Lt. General Thorat's visit had interesting side lights. He called on Maj. General (Retd.) Masters who was chief of the city's town services. General Masters would invariably use the epithet 'bloody' which really meant nothing to him. General Thorat had worked in a junior capacity with General Masters: so when the former called on the latter, pat came the query from General Masters, as to how the bloody, Mem Saheb of General Thorat was ? Thorat seemed to colour a little in the face and then realised the style of General Masters' address.

Ananda Mayee Ma, a saintly lady from Benaras (Varanasi) was camping at Ranchi when the TISCO trouble took place. Ananda Mayee Ma is a greatly respected figure. She is believed to have blessed Mrs. Indira Gandhi and given her a charmed string of beads. Ma was delivering religious discourses in the local temple newly put up by her disciples. She would go for a drive in the evening but would not go inside any private residence. My wife would meet her at the gate. When she reported to Ma about my long absence at Jamshedpur in connection with the labour agitation, Ma told my wife that a big conflagration was going on there with a large number of houses set on fire. This was the day when the shanty market was set ablaze ! The clairvoyance of Ma struck the people as quite amazing and my wife repeated this incident to all her friends.

The scheme for setting up a heavy engineering corporation at Ranchi with a gigantic foundry and forging unit was being planned then. There was no provision in the blue print for the general administrative set up including that of the police ! The mistakes which had been committed at Sindri nearly ten years ago were being repeated. Any laxity in the law and order aspect would militate against the effective setting up of the plant, but there was lethargy and complacence all round. Later serious communal trouble and even subversion activity cropped up here due to this mistake.

The Ranchi scene showed a simmer of discontent amongst the Adivasis, the pristine tribes inhabiting Chhota Nagpur plateau for centuries. A section of them known as Tana Bhagats was more vociferous. They had pulled in favour of the Congress movement during the earlier regime in spite of the ministration to the contrary of the missionaries, who were used as the pincer group of the country's administration. Tana Bhagats had avoided being proselytised. They would take out mammoth processions from time to time giving vent to their discontent with the administrative set up and asking for concessions specially as they had suffered in the national movement and had worked shoulder to shoulder with the more educated and sophisticated Congress workers from the plains. The Tanas were sanctioned small pensions but this could hardly satisfy them The problem appears to be still unsolved and is an item in favour of the setting up of a separate hill state in the eastern sector of the country carved out from Bihar, West Bengal, Orissa, Madhya Pradesh and even some portions of Andhra Pradesh.

The inauguration of the first factory in the country for manufacturing explosives for use in mining operations at Gomia in Hazaribagh district was a major event. This factory was in fact the first of its kind in Asia and was put up by the Imperial Chemical Industries of U.K., which have ramifications the world over. The inauguration was performed by the President of India Dr. Rajendra Prasad and the top brass of the Imperial Chemical Industries came along to join the ceremony. The board of directors was headed by a British peer. Led by him the cavalcade came via Calcutta in airconditioned railway coaches. All of them preferred to stay in these carriages while the President of India was accommodated in the local guest house which was done up to some extent to receive him. Yet the reception arrangements for their own bosses by the I.C.I. officers and those for the President of India, showed marked difference and indicated the old colonial mentality. It was after a certain amount of coaxing that the officers of the Imperial Chemical Industries could be persuaded to see sense and take care of all the formal courtesies to be paid to the Head of State in the country. The fireworks show put up on the occasion was memorable and the explosive factory management boastfully advertised that this was one of the very best in any part of the world. Doubtless the show outclassed the best seen in the Delhi Durbar and even the princely order could not boast of such a demonstration even though they would go to any length in making such an impression. Clad in simple Indian dress the President made a very impressive showing. He spoke briefly at the inauguration and eulogised the I.C.I for all they had done. I am sure the Directors of I.C.I. felt humbled.

Prime Minister Nehru performed the opening ceremony of the Maithon Dam, one of a series of four put up on the Damodar river, the river of sorrow for a large part of the States of Bihar and West Bengal. Maithon was the third dam in the series. The Prime Minister insisted on the opening ceremony being performed by one of the labourers (an Adivasi woman) who was employed on the construction of the dam. This was more in accord with the style suited to our country, and has been repeated since. The visit of the Prime Minister to the dam site—he stayed overnight at the local guest house, had some interesting facets. He landed at Panagarh near Asansol in an I.A.F. aircraft. Earlier the Chief Minister of West Bengal Dr. B.C. Roy also came in a state government plane to Panagarh to receive the Prime Minister and so did the Chief Minister of Bihar, Babu Sri Krishan Singh. Dr. B.C. Roy utilised his travels in the State government aricraft, for indulging in his favourite game of bridge. His Principal Secretary was always specially selected from the official cadre of those who could play this game well. Dr. Roy stayed on in the aircraft even after it had landed, merely to finish the hand which was being played ! Conveyance from the airport to Maithon presented a fairly formidable problem of protocol as both the Chief Ministers had to be accommodated in the same car and they had to show themselves to the populace along with the Prime Minister. This was not feasible as the car had to carry the P.M.'s personal security staff as well. The difficulty was sorted out by the Bengal Chief Minister sitting with the P.M. in his car, and at the border the change over took place. The Chief Minister of Bihar remained sitting in a second car during the journey in West Bengal. The units visited en-route included the Bharat Aluminium Works at J.K. Nagar. This factory, a pioneer in many ways, got into the red and had to be closed down, palpably due to labour trouble, but the reasons were greatly different. The visit did not help in sorting out the nascent troubles. Later the Panchet Dam was also dedicated to the nation in a similar ceremony but learning from experience the P.M. came to the site in a state government aircraft from Patna and returned to Delhi the same day from there on the bigger I.A.F. plane.

Road Transport had assumed special importance in this hilly terrain specially as railway tracks were not so numerous. A Regional Transport Authority was there as for the other divisions in the state, to take decisions on issuance of permits for trucks, buses and taxies. This was a position of patronage in a government racketting in licences and permits. The members on the body were carefully nominated by government and included either politicians beaten at the polls, or those who missed getting a party nomination. At least three of the members nominated at this time were later to become prominent ministers in the state cabinet. This forum was well known as a seed bed of corruption and factional politics. The cronies sitting on the Board revelled in obtaining guidance from the minister concerned on even small matters. On a surprise check on the Dhanbad road I was mortified to find that a licenced bus, which should carry forty persons, was carrying a load of more than a hundred adults and a large cargo of goats and chicken, all inside the body of the vehicle. The licence holder was reported against and was only severely reprimanded by the Transport Authority. When the case went to a court of law, it was hotly contested by the licence holder who made out that so many people, and goats and poultry could not be accommodated in the limited space available. The case ended in conviction after some time but I did not have the protection of the court that I had when I had brought the case against the taxi-driver in the court at Patna. The lawyer for the defence indulged in unsavoury gimmicks to prove that I was wrong. A taxi was also found by me about this time to be carrying more than two dozen persons including a few in its luggage boot. The driver carried a passenger under him and another on top of himself as well. An interesting interlude in an otherwise monotonous touring but the cross-examination in court in the connected case was to say the least, objectionable and nothing could be done about it. The fine imposed had no deterrent value. Traffic control and check work was a veritable gold mine to the police authorities at the spot and nothing appeared to rectify it.

The forested areas in the Chhota Nagpur belt were a favourite spot for shikaris and shooting parties were arranged on payment by firms headquartered mainly at Calcutta. It was customary to reserve a Block for a specific period and get various parties to do the shooting. Later the shooting of the tiger was banned as the licence system lead to huge decimation of the canine species. A brother-in-law of the then Inspector General of Police, an army officer, was on a visit to one of these areas and shikar was arranged for him by the local Superintendent of Police near Dalton Ganj, headquarters of the district of Palamau. The Superintendent of Police arranged a *machan* and all the ancillaries for the I.G.'s brother-in-law and himself mounted the *machan* with him. However, he would not let the brother-in-law do the shooting as the S.P. said he was frightened that the tiger may attack the *machan*. About twenty years earlier a Deputy Commissioner of the district Mr. Bakshi of the I.C.S., who thought he had downed a tiger, left the *machan* to see what had happened. He was severely mauled but the tiger was luckily disposed of by another shikari who had gone with the Deputy Commissioner for the reconnaissance. The Superintendent of Police had, therefore, arranged that the shooting may be done from some other *machan* on behalf of the I.G.'s brother-in-law, and in case of a successful shot, it would be claimed that the I.G.'s relation had bagged the tiger! He made the bland statement that if anything adverse happened, what explanation would be offered to his boss—*Unko kya muh dikhain ge.*

Shooting in this area did not show up because it involved expenditure which few could afford. Yet it was necessary to impart the skill of shooting with fire arms to the middle class people. The poorer people in the villages did keep a large number of muzzle loaders, some of which were licensed, and used the weapons for protection of life and property. But in the town, where the middle classes generally lived, this was not the case and very few guns and fire arms were available. Even gun licence holders, were known never to have fired a round from the weapon held by them. I had the mortification of finding that one of the local businessmen, who had also been the President of the Chamber of Commerce both at the state level and the divisional level, and had a large number of licensed fire arms, some of which could be kept by his retainers for protecting his house and property, was himself quite alien to the art of shooting. If this was his state, the less affluent people's plight could be imagined. Therefore, I considered that a rifle shooting association should be organised for this area. This had a ready response and it was a gala event when this association held the general meeting once a year. The forum provided good public relations for the police. On this occasion some shooting with small caliber weapons and also by revolvers was resorted to at the range. During his tenure as the Rajyapal of the state, Dr. Zakir Hussain presided over these functions as he was always in his summer camp at Ranchi. On the first occasion when he came to preside over this function in 1957, it was arranged that he would fire from a .22 bore rifle set on a tripod. His shot was to release a mass of balloons as it went through the bull's eye where the main fastening of the balloons was laid. As Dr. Zakir Hussain fired the shot from the tripod, the baloons soared up. A Pathan, he asserted candidly that this was his very first shot from a gun and he was happy that it had hit the bull's eye ! It was my disappointment that only when a visit by a V.I.P. was arranged, many people turned up to witness the *tamasha* and also participate, but otherwise the facilities offered were not used. On one occasion the prize distribution ceremony, which was arranged separately, had to be gone through with a State Deputy Minister presiding. He was no attraction and therefore except for the prize winners there was no audience whatsoever available. Even some of the prize winners were not to be found. Therefore the audience had to be collected by a device very much like the one which was adopted earlier on the visit of the Prime Minister to Patna. The Deputy Minister would also have been very unhappy with a small gathering. This meeting syndrome has been the bane of political V.I.Ps in the country.

About this time, there was a revolt by the Kharwars in the District of Palamau. They declared themselves independent, little realising that a democratic republic existed in the country. They had in fact, not liked the visitation by village level government officials and considered that they should be spared from their exactions. Both visiting police personnel and Panchayat workers were fired at. The proclamation of independence was nailed in local lingo on the trees. Full scale operations with a large body of military police thrown in, could cow them down. Almost the entire population of Kharwars was placed in the District jail but later they were given pardon. A special scheme for their upliftment was taken in hand.

Ranchi boasted of a Regional Tribal Research Institute headed by a retired director of the Anthropological Survey of India, Dr. Guha. Dr. Verrier Elwin was an old associate of Dr. Guha and paid many visits to Ranchi. He had conducted special studies amongst the tribals in Madhya Pradesh and even in Orissa in the areas where I had been posted. Dr. Guha arranged for the visit of some tribal chieftains from the then NEFA, now designated as Arunachal Pradesh. These tribal chiefs indicated to me their decision to be left alone as far as possible so that the poor denizens of their estates did not have to suffer at the hands of corrupt subordinates specially of the police. This applied to a good chunk of the Chhota Nagpur plateau also though it had better accessibility and was higher in the scale of development. Yet there was no reason why these tribals should not be allowed to develop their own personality. As in the case of Kharwar this was termed as a desire on their part to get self governing institutions, free from the influence of the plainsmen *dikkus* (foreigners) as they were termed. The government policy had been to undo the tribal institutions, in spite of the advice given by Verrier Elwin and Dr. Guha. The village headman, who mattered, had been divested of his powers and prestige in a bid to introduce a centralised police like the one existing in the plains in Bihar. This made the administration wooden and cut off from the grassroots. It increased the cost to the public exchequer, without commensurate benefit. The centralised system introduced a procedure of exaction. One story had it that a police constable on patrol in a village demanded money when a child died as he said this was due to the neglect by the family members. It should have been reported. In the case of birth, a fee was asked for as prior notice of a likely birth should be given in the same way as it was necessary to send intimation to the police of all cases of death which may be unnatural or suspicious. The main item on the government's list, however, was how to enlist the tribals' support in future elections. The tribals were greatly under the influence of Christian missionaries who had done them good service in large pockets. To counter the missionaries was indeed difficult and this was considered necessary in view of the subversion allied to them in other areas like Nagaland. Indeed it was necessary to usher in secular, welfare organisations to pander to the basic requirements of the people. But would this be done ?

The Heavy Engineering Corporation works at Ranchi, put up with Russian and Czechoslovak cooperation, came in for attention at the hands of subversive elements. There was a big blaze in a godown bay which put the hands back by about six months. The ill equipped factory had no fire brigade worth the name and units had to be called out from Asansol in West Bengal and from Patna, the State capital. The investigation disclosed the ramifications of pro-Pakistan elements. A fairly complicated conspiracy case was made out and the central intelligence organisations lent a hand in the work. This was about the time when there was a recrudescence of the old Hindu-Muslim problem, perhaps engineered by the same subversive group, to sow seeds of confusion. First there was rioting in the Ranchi main bazar which was quelled promptly but a series of riots took place about a year later which covered the Heavy Engineering Corporation's housing complex and also the Ranchi township. These caused considerable loss to the minority community. A Commission of Enquiry headed by a retired

Supreme Court Judge, Mr Justice Dayal, was set up. The report focussed attention on the deficiencies of the police. However, there has been no change worth the name in the police set up.

The structure of administration with the District Magistrate and the Superintendent of Police, who generally did not see eye to eye with each other now, was proving inadequate. Even at the divisional level the revenue authorities headed by the Divisional Commissioner and the police headed by the Deputy Inspector General carried on much the same tale as was applicable to the district sphere. At the same time the police force was now identified as the force behind the party or group in power. The armed force was gaining strength while the unarmed wing was languishing. The armed policemen, to be used on special occasions, were now used up almost entirely for mounting guard on the residence of VIPs and for escorting them in their trips about the country side. They were even utilised for enforcing the personal will of the members of the power group. The mounting strength of the armed wing showed that the government was not popular and that the will of the state required to be enforced by armed might. What could be done by an unarmed constable earlier would now require a fully armed section of men. This armed wing, though previously a small parcel of the civil police, now exemplified the earlier police better than the constable in the police station, who did not carry any fire arms. There were cases of dispute between neighbouring states, for example U.P. and Bihar, where the armed police was ranged on either side in support of the revenue department officials. A similar situation prevailed on the Nepal border, and police had to be rushed there even though there was no history of a border dispute between Nepal and any state in India thus far. In the case of differences between the states of Bihar and Orissa over the inclusion of Seraikela and Kharsawan in either state on one occasion the armed police of Orissa marched in with drums and bugles signifying their victory and inclusion of the area in that state, while later it was the Bihar armed police which dealt with the situation in a similar manner. Such incidents did not give any credit to the police and showed them as a successor to the colonial army of occupation and not the police which the people were looking forward to. The armed police were now being given higher caliber weapons, and even the training pattern was suited to guerrillas, this when there was no insurgency in the country at all !

While this was the state of the police, discussions in the State Assembly showed that the item in which the legislature was concerned par excellence was to recount some instances of corruption of police subordinates or their alleged collusion with political bosses. The police force was getting politicised and was getting further away from their normal goals. There was no sense of priority at the policy making levels.

The reorganisation of the armed police had resulted in putting up what was known as military police battalions on the lines of artillery units in the army. Each unit consisted of four to five effective companies with a headquarters complement. Each company was in its turn divided into three platoons, which in turn had three sections each consisting of about ten effective personnel. Although originally the special armed police in the state was of the order of about six or seven companies, now as many and even more battalions were put up. The number of these battalions was ever-increasing and within a period of about five to six years their number was further doubled. This resulted in earmarking special units to cater for special training facilities, which were lacking. But all this followed the old conventional lines, and there was no attempt to fashion the training to the changing requirements particularly the recrudescence of communal trouble and the development of insurrectionism based on the economic imbalance in the country. Even though these units were expected to perform the duties of a special task force, it was interesting that posting to these units was made of the rejects. Thus a vicious circle was started and the new units started becoming more and more ineffective. The picture in the central sphere was much the same where the armed reserve meant for the political agents of the British period were grouped into battallions and were designated as the Central Reserve Police. The objective of this force was to assist the administration in the centrally administered areas in normal work and also to provide reserves for assistance to the states, whose demand for armed force was insatiable. The C.R.P.F. had become a small army. This served to obviate the necessity of calling in the army for assistance but the indications were that a separate law and order armed constabulary was needed. A host of miscellaneous armed forces were also set up at the central level for specific jobs like guarding of new public sector industries and their installations, keeping vigil over the borders, and even providing protection on the railways. Their organisational pattern required a re-think.

The rigging up of armed police units synchronised with a more stringent control over the Indian Police Service. The Indian Police Service officers had to some extent a schizophrenic existence. There were numerous cases when the state ministers, suspicious of the doings of these officers, had them removed peremptorily from the state sphere. In some cases this acted greatly to the disadvantage of these officers, who were neither owned by the centre nor by the states. Thus the morale of the All India Police Service went down sharply. With larger recruitment, the general standard of the recruits had already gone down. Some studies were made of this question but these adorned the archives of the state and nothing was done to rectify the defects.

The police in the states was more and more identified with local goings on and were a pet subject of political pulls. Successive general elections also indicate that the people were guided entirely by local considerations. Apparently the country was making no progress on the path to democracy and the police force was becoming increasingly attached to the apron strings of the political machine. There was a marked deterioration in morale and in standards of work and performance. The capacity of the senior officers to withstand political interference, was nil.

As this time a District Superintendent of Police, who considered himself to be the favourite of the ruling group, threw out a challenge to the District Magistrate to arrest a denizen of a neighbouring state as he had the temerity to criticise the sons of the soil and the administration of the state ! The District Magistrate had to cajole the District Superintendent and calm him down. The S.P.'s act would have perhaps created an inter-state problem ! This denizen of a neighbouring state had merely stated in the presence of the S.P. that the local people had no stamina and because of their laziness they were left behind in the race for development. He had also stated that the state administration was lax. The S.P. wanted to show his closeness to the Chief Minister and his concern for the reputation of the local populace. His performance generally was highly dismal and it ill behoved him to take up offensive in this manner. Another district officer sported the portrait of the Chief Minister, the presiding deity of the state, on all the four walls in the sitting room of his residence. It was his firm belief that those who would visit his residence would consider him as the chief's disciple—*chela*—who whichever side he turned saw only the mentor's image. Doubtless this would be conveyed to the boss and such personality worship would earn him rich dividends. Indeed this happened, and sitting under the shadow of the portrait, he was known to have indulged in numerous irregularities but the vigilance department of the state could not make him the object of their investigations!

The police were now used for all odd jobs. In the British regime it was the sole channel of general administration but in the new democracy there was nothing which was not covered in their charter of duties. There was a case in which a close relation of the Chief Minister suddenly disappeared from his residence and a hue and cry was raised, affecting the normal working of the administrative sections of the state in each district. The prime job now was to trace the missing boy. Ultimately this young person was located in the neighbouring state of West Bengal staying in an ignominious manner. There was a clear indication of the direction in which the wind was blowing. The administration was fast declining to the subjective rule of the Nawabs. There was also a noticeable effect on the moral standards. In particular the receiving of illegal gratification became a routine matter and this was nonchalantly ascribed to the rise in prices. The ideas about the standards of living had started getting reoriented upward while there was a distinct march forward to poverty. A race appeared to have started between businessmen and those in government employ for higher living. The business community would pander to the taste of the officialdom as the latter had control over the issuing of permits and licences, which made for most of the businessman's earnings. Consequently junior officers were found possessing cars, refrigerators and air conditioners though the value of their salary in terms of purchasing power had gone down. The pay scales of the new incumbents, at least in the superior services, were much lower. Even police constables went about gaudily dressed and their get togethers were now celebrated with considerable pomp and show while in the earlier days these were inexpensive. The businessman also engaged greatly in exercises pandering to the comfort of the flesh and sordid stories of the happenings were going the rounds. In the club at Ranchi, drinking was on a large scale and it was amusing to see specially the bosses of public sector undertakings being regaled with scotch most liberally, both hands holding filled glasses—served at somebody else's cost.

The trend in corruption techniques at the police grass-roots level came to my notice through a retired Deputy Inspector General, a denizen of the state, who had a family farm in north Bihar in the district of Monghyr. Posted at Patna, he was informed by his farm manager of a dispute that had developed on the land with a neighbour in regard to the demarcation of the land boundary. Earlier during the colonial set-up, the landlords—zamindars as they were called in the State—would make a monthly payment to the officer-in-charge of the police station for giving timely assistance in case this was needed in a routine manner. That meant that the landlord had the upper hand in all land disputes. But this monthly subsidy was not levied from officials of the government for obvious reasons. Generally speaking government officials got assistance for obtaining their rightful claims. With the acquisition of zamindaris, this routine income was reported to have been denied to the police station staff. Now each item required its own quota of graft. So when the farm manager approached the officer-in-charge of the police station, he was informed that assistance was possible on appropriate payment. The Deputy Inspector General informed the local Police Superintendent and though the police station staff, duly cautioned, promised to go into action, this was deliberately delayed. And this would mean delay in the sowing operations with consequential loss to the Deputy Inspector General. Fearing this, the farm manager entered into a deal with the officer-in-charge and could get assistance at "concessional rate", as the land belonged to the Deputy Inspector General. He later informed his boss and the latter had to acquiesce in it. The incident showed that greasing of the wheels of administration by such subterfuge was an unavoidable item, however, repugnant it may be to the honest citizen. Nothing could be done about it, unless there was a violent revolution which would uproot the existing procedures completely. This alone could expose the perpetrators of this perfidy and invite a social revenge that would make such action worthless. The interesting aspect about this incident was the assertion of the police officer at the police station that he had agreed to a smaller sum changing hands as the person concerned was a senior member of the police force and was perhaps known to the officer-in-charge also !

There was a chain of divisional commissioners during my tenure at Ranchi. One of them was an officer promoted from the state civil service. He retired after a very brief stint at Ranchi. Sometime later he paid a visit to Ranchi to enlist my assistance for getting his pension papers sorted out. He had taken care to submit these papers to the state government on the eve of his retirement. The Accountant General's office at Ranchi, would not give the final clearance. I was happy when he met me a few days later and reported that the papers had been finalised. But that was not the entire story. He gleefully said that he had passed on about five hundred rupees to the incumbents in the pension section of the A.G's office and thereafter it had been smooth sailing. He came out with another interesting statement that he considered government working efficient as despite difficulties—the State finances being in the red—and the red tape, we continued to get the monthly salary bill through !

The Deputy Director of Health Services at Ranchi was somewhat of a martinent but he had an equal number in the rank of compounders, who dealt with his boss violently. Feeling greatly humiliated the Deputy Director went to the Superintendent of Police to lodge a complaint. The Superintendent of Police was reported to be indisposed, and he reacted somewhat differently. He advised the doctor to lodge his complaint at the police station where appropriate action could be taken. This dignitary, however, wanted the Superintendent of Police to swing into action personally or through a senior officer. He contacted me on the phone and when I enquired of the details from the Superintendent, the latter intimated that whenever he required some medical assistance and contacted the Deputy Director, he was told to go to the casualty officer or some junior functionary. Generally the medicine took weeks to be supplied. The Superintendent of Police wanted the Deputy Director of Health Services to obtain police help in a similar manner. The argument was hardly convincing but in view of the Superintendent of Police's indisposition, minor though it was, I directed the Deputy Superintendent of Police to see to the investigation of the incident which indeed involved flagrant violation of discipline and attracted some sections of the Indian Penal Code as well. In any case the Superintendent of Police's assertion about the lethargy of the Health Department functionaries, was entirely correct and showed how a vital wing of the government's social services was operating. You could do nothing about it except make a hullaboo, which the Superintendent of Police had raised correctly. I told off the Deputy Director but this did not register with him. Later huge defalcations in this department's offices were detected and the S.P. who was in charge of the investigations, had took it out on the doctors with a characteristic bang. This was a self righteous pose from the local police as a little later huge embezzelment from the motor vehicles taxation wing of the S.P's office also came to light. This S.P. was squarely responsible for this mismanagement even though he may not have been personally involved. Although I had pointed out some lacunae, this officer had not acted promptly and so the defalcation. There was the same story of neglect all round and the rot was going deeper into the system.

During this period I could manage to go to the countries of eastern Asia including Japan on a holiday. The efficiency of the Japanese policeman was striking and as for discipline, I was informed that the rules permitted an unarmed police constable on parade, being admonished by a slap or a kick if he was found slack. In India, the police constable had to be shown special respect and yet he hardly gave an indication of being the member of a disciplined service. The malady had affected the senior ranks as well. This was entirely due to the political climate in the country. The biggest casualty was punctuality. I was ashamed to find fairly senior officers coming late to the functions organised even at the Raj Bhavan. When this was pointed out, the only reaction obtained was that I was a fault finder and a remnant of the British steel frame. It was time I mended my ways !

The P & O Liner in which we travelled touched at Chittagong in East Pakistan (now in Bangladesh). Only a few days earlier Col. Bhattacharya an Indian officer was caught allegedly in Pakistani territory over which quite a controversy had been built up. A friend from Patna, now living in Chittagong, provided fellowship to us for the day at Chittagong. The confusion there appeared to me reassuring as we in India had a better and more orderly existence. When I returned to the ship at night, safe and sound, my host and I heaved a sigh of relief. My host told me that my completely private visit could have been misconstrued and I may have been in trouble. The police in East Pakistan were a back number though and it was the army which ruled the roost. I saw here a memorable sight, the washing ashore about a mile away from the shore line, of a twelve thousand ton passenger vessel. The ship was locked in sand in an upright position. The Government of Pakistan wanted to use this vessel as a tourist hotel, but Chittagong was not a tourist draw—not even for this peculiar sight—and the ship was later dismantled. In Burma the conditions were still worse and right in Rangoon, all houses functioned as mini forts, with grills and steel gates fixed along the outer periphery. A few miles out of Rangoon and there was a very reasonable chance of any one being faced by insurgents. The scene here also gave a favourable picture of affairs back at home. But further east in Malaysia, Singapore, Hongkong, Thailand, and in Japan the conditions were much better. Life was more placid and enjoyable. The police acted effectively and had the confidence of the people. The policeman's place in the social scale was fairly high. A boost for the Indian police appeared necessary but the dangers were that with the economy still on the poorer side, the gap between the people and the police would widen and act to the detriment of all police operations. There was, however, no doubt about the poor equipment of the police—there were no control rooms worth the name—but a small place like Penang in the Malaysian peninsula had a well equipped control-room and its ancillaries.

Little interest was taken by the intelligentsia in matters connected with crime prevention but even a minor incident was magnified out of all proportion and was broadcast in the press as a case of the establishment's inefficiency. I wished to harness the critical crowd for making practical suggestions. A crime prevention society which could also hold a library, a research unit, and some public relations outfit, was set going in Ranchi. The Rajyapal, Dr. Zakir Hussian, always interested in such constructive exercises, became the patron of this organisation. Very useful discussions, particularly on the slant of the tribal areas on crime causation and rehabilitation of the offenders, took place and Dr. Zakir Hussain lent his guidance. I was, however, shocked to see the apathy in the establishment for this move which was characterised as a propaganda platform set up by some police officers. U.P. had a similar organisation rigged up by the brother of Shri Sampurnanand one time Chief Minister of U.P., Shri Paripurnanand and it was getting on reasonably well. I failed to find a counterpart to Shri Paripurnanand in the state of Bihar.

This society which was set up at great personal sacrifice closed down when I got transferred to Patna. Paripurnanand later visited Patna and informed me that his organisation had little political support but he had rigged up a band of devoted workers, who kept it up. Paripurnanand had a fantastic memory for figures of crime etc., and his approach to the criminals was entirely from the angle of a reformer. How I wished something could be done in Bihar too !

After Ranchi I had a stint of posting in the C.I.D., Crime wing. The C.I.D. was essentially the base of administration in the British days. And the same pattern continued. It appeared that the information collected through this agency was greatly impartial and unbiased. The political elements which provided information to their leaders in the past, were now removed from their old ideals of service and appeared to be taking sides. The information furnished by the C.I.D. was therefore found increasingly useful by the Government. But here too the politician was making inroads, though yet not on top. This intelligence wing was required now to watch some members of the ruling party who came under a cloud. This was an assignment bristling with difficulties. But I was in charge of the wing in the C.I.D. which dealt with criminals and this aspect of work did not touch me. The Crime wing did not appear to have attracted much attention. Even the Crime wing of old was a dread force and it had built up an image of an all-knowing group. However, it was a disappointment for me to find its present performance. Personal standards had deteriorated and there was no indication of adopting new styles. New gadgets which could fill in the gap were not in evidence. I made a study of this and placed an indent for some modern equipment. I wanted to experiment with lie detectors, and the truth serum, the last item had been utilised to some extent in the hospital for mental diseases at Ranchi. It was necessary for legal and procedural matters to be delved into about the truth serum. But by and large there was no enthusiasm for this exercise. It was interesting that the state finance department raised the query as to how investigation work could be managed so long in the state without the gadgets now asked for ! They noted that it was not necessary to get the new fangled equipment.

Adulteration of petrol and hoarding of foodstuffs had become the order of the day. Both these items had been handled in an admirable way in Punjab. An attempt was, therefore, made to make a drive against adulteration of petrol on the lines adopted in Punjab. Samples of petrol from the various pumps in the state were taken simultaneously for examination. But it was an uphill task having these samples tested for the flash point to determine how much of adulteration, if any, was in evidence. This simple matter took months and after considerable difficulty a special unit for these tests could be set up in the state Forensic Science Laboratory. Till then the cases remained pending causing considerable discontent. In regard to the hoarding of foodstuffs as also their adulteration there was hardly any let-up although under an empirical order a large number of persons were taken in custody and detained. This created a reign of terror; there was much political criticism and ultimately the entire lot of detenus had to be released. The position came back to square one.

There was a visit to the state by the then Chief Minister of Punjab—Comrade Ram Kishan, ostensibly for arranging supplies of some foodgrains to the state on a state to state basis. Comrade Ram Kishan headed the government in the truncated Punjab in India, which had not yet been vivisected. He was a humble worker from West Punjab, and was specially selected by the Congress leadership for this job for his rectitude and dedication to duty. His term unfortunately was short lived as his election was later set aside by an electoral court. He has since gone into the wilderness. At Patna, he addressed a meeting of the local Punjabi Biradri, which was attended by the State Chief Minister K.B. Sahay. The Biradri was planning to build a hall and allied facilities on land which was available, in memory of Lala Lajpat Rai. Comrade Saheb exhorted the Bihar C.M. to help as the latter was also the state head of the Lajpat Memorial Fund Committee headed at the Centre by Lal Bahadur Shastri, a member of Lalaji's Servants of the People Society. K.B. Sahay, after a heavy engagement on the day, went to sleep comfortably while the Comrade went on with his exhortation to the Punjabi community to identify themselves with the local inhabitants. When he woke up and was requested to speak as well, he did not know what to say and simply affirmed his support for all that had been stated by Comrade Saheb of which he was unaware. Result : he collected a hundred thousand rupees for the Lajpat Rai Memorial Fund. The treasurer of the Biradri's Lajpat Rai Memorial Committee, contacted Shri Sahay and what was his surprise when he was handed over a heap of currency notes tied up in a duster lying in a corner of Shri Sahay's office room atop a chest of drawers. K.B. Sahay had a penchant for collection of funds. These collections were dumped in old corners to be handed over to those for whom these were intended. Unorthodox though his ways were, I believe his personal objectives and intentions were generally clean. In politics he was considered to be a slippery figure. He was charge-sheeted later for corrupt practices but died in a car accident during the pendency of the case in court. I believe there was not adequate evidence against him.

K.B. Sahay had ordered the detention of a large number of dealers in foodgrains etc., to teach them a lesson in rectitude and the principle that moderate profits as permitted should be made and not the loot which appeared to be the order of the day. In this drive he had appeared to be harsh and empirical. He wanted even the connected bureaucracy to fall in line with him. The idea of a result-oriented administration was his goal as K.B. Sahay found that conventional methods were proving an utter failure in our democracy, in which the emphasis was only on rights and little on the sacrifices required for a good social order. Corruption had gone into the very system of work, and therefore his thesis was to take up cudgels against blatant acts rather than take steps which may even clog the wheels of administration. This appeared to be a very sensible approach to the mounting problems even though it was impossible to spell it out publicly in a society where prudery had come to have pride of place. These standards applied to the police whole hog but who would bell the cat ? Otherwise methodical in his ways and with a perspective plan before him, I found K.B. Sahay's ideas rather archaic and inappropriate in more ways than one. He would readily agree to any amount of extra expenditure to be incurred by the establishment. His pet thesis was that the state governments could afford to have a deficit budget and it was for the Government of India to bridge the gap, whatever it be. He was very fond of early morning walks whereafter he would settle down in his office room to shave. He would transact quite a lot of official business at this hour in his office room at the residence. I was summoned on many an occasion to his office at this hour. I argued with him to hold this session if he so desired in his dressing room which was apter for such exercises. But he stuck to his guns. This unorthodox behaviour had repercussions on the rank and file in the administration as well. I believe even district officers and District Police Superintendents started acting in this fashion, which was indeed not conducive to creating a healthy precedent.

A crime prevention exhibition was organised about this time to focus the attention of the people in general on what was expected from the common citizen whenever an offence was discovered and what could be done by the police. This exhibition showed ways of house breaking, lock breaking etc. and how these could be countered. There were cases of forged coins and currency notes and also the methods of countering dacoities. While this exhibition was a great success, it was unfortunate that in the department itself there was more than one opinion about its usefulness. It appeared that the other wings of the police were jealous of the popularity of the C.I.D., criminal investigation wing. I also drew up a detailed scheme for using the Home Guards, the newly organised force, for control of crimes. The Home Guards organisation itself resisted being utilised for this work ! On analysing it, I found that the police officers located in the Home Guards organisation had aligned themselves to a political sub-group of the ruling party. And this group wanted to confine activities on the level which would attract votes in future elections. They did not want the Home Guards to become a second line police force, as this force (Police) was already aligned with the dominant group in the ruling party. Sensing this, the ministerial portfolios were also changed later to undo the wrong that had been done ! The Press carried bold headlines on these issues but it appeared that rather than mend their policy of action, the government wanted to control the Press. In this connection advertisements released to the Press by various government agencies came up for a good deal of comment as these were now denied to the papers that did not toe the official line. The position was indeed interesting but unedifying.

10

ARMED POLICE

THERE was an interesting assignnent in the police department in Bihar designated as D.I.G., Armed Forces and Training. In addition to his normal duties, this officer was also in charge of the Home Guards and the Fire Services of the state. This D.I.G. exercised jurisdiction over Home Guards work as the Commandant General of this Force and in this capacity he was not subordinated to the Inspector General of Police. Amusingly this officer was in the abbreviated terminology termed as D.I.G. *Afat*. Later the designation was charged to D.I.G. M.P. and T. i.e. Military Police and Training. I was posted to this job for about a year.

It was interesting that with a Military Police force under him of over ten battalions, the D I.G. had no office staff organisation. The armed component of the district police continued to exist and outnumbered the Military Police which, better armed than the district armed police, was to function as a reserve to be deployed in an emergency. However, in effect almost the entire military police force was deployed in the districts of which the S.P. became the local commandant. The battalion commandants had a cushy time, looking after the general management of his body of men while the S.P. revelled in using them as he liked to substitute his own men, whose number particularly in the armed wing was found increasingly insufficient. I prepared standard battalion orders for application to military police units in order to rationalize their working. But the prime challenge was the expansion of the Military Police. We had to suddenly expand this force by about five battalions, this to counter the need for using Central Reserve Police force units. The appellation Military Police brought titters in the army circles as this formation had a special place of its own in the set-up of army units. They policed the members of the army units and ensured that they kept within bounds. However, the similarity in the set-ups of the military unit and the military police had resulted in christening this force accordingly. There was even a separate act regarding the functioning of military police units of the police department inherited from Bengal and this was copied out as the Bihar Military Police Act. It bore provisions for the disciplinary code of the sepoy and higher ranks, which was nearly on all fours with the army units while in their barracks in the cantonments. The "Army Act" had provisions for situations of actual warfare which would not find place in the enactment meant for the police.

The expansion was required to be made without provisions of additional barracks or office accommodation and the entire process appeared to be concentrating on the aspect of making appointments ; the politicians vied with each other in inducting their proteges in this force. I attempted to introduce regional recruitment to have a balance of all the areas in the state and also to provide adequate place to the weaker sections of the community without in any manner reducing standards. I believed in having really capable and fit men to man the posts in the force, but the entire process was hustled through and even some senior recruiting police officers were reported to have made a packet. My job for some time was therefore to keep tabs on these functionaries, and no body would care a whit about the quality of the men recruited.

The training of this new force was a problem to be contended with as the existing institutions were already full with routine material. Temporary training centres had to be set up under canvas and the items included training in the mechanics of bivouac and jungle warfare ! This was quite unnecessary but had to be done as desired by the government. The half trained units had to undertake route marches. One of the commandants, required to march with his men, reported having done so when he had barely started with them and after staying en route at an inspection house, joined the men at the destination about ten days later, travelling by car. He was found out and had to be taken to task but he found political supporters who helped him out with only a reprimand administered to him. In his defence he made out the story of having fallen ill en route for which he fabricated false evidence. Such behaviour on the part of a young I.P.S. officer caused some eyebrow raising in the Secretariat. What was disappointing was the support and interest evinced in his case by politicians and senior bureaucrats including police officers who belonged to his caste.

The battalions of this armed force should have been accommodated in separate locations for each unit with the complement of office, stores, armoury, and allied buildings. However, this was nowhere near attainment and efforts were afloat to take over disused army encampments or places for accommodating displaced persons, even food godowns. Even these took years to rig up while the men were put out on duty. This system of putting the cart before the horse was typical of our administrative methods. This force could not get its pay in time resulting in desertions and some discontent among those who stuck on. The seeds of dissatisfaction were being sown in this force and the trend was the same in other states. This method of work resulted a few years later in a mutiny in the P.A.C., of U.P. The Bihar Military Police was spared this travail, thanks to Pt. Ramanand Tiwary, who introduced a dose of sanity in them. He was soon to become the Home Minister of the state.

I had to work till late hours in office. Leaving office for lunch one day I discovered that I had left my Parker pen on my office table. When I returned I found the pen missing. Apparently this could not have happened without the connivance of the office orderly, a sepoy of the Bihar military police. No trace of the pen could be found and therefore, I recorded a note in the service book of this orderly that his conduct was not satisfactory. I was surprised, however, to receive a telephone call from an important minister (a co-casteman of the sepoy), asking if I had recorded an adverse entry in the service book of the sepoy and why it could not be cancelled. This sepoy was a Bhumihar. As I refused to make any amendment in the remarks and enquired from the minister how he could learn of such an entry, which is an insignificant matter of official routine, he took umbrage and designated me in the political circles as anti-Bhumihar. Apparently constables were having direct access to ministers of their own caste. Though the new recruitment was made in accordance with government orders, of which I did not approve, this minister interestingly wanted the C.M. to enquire how many Rajputs were enlisted for the new battalions and how it compared with the intake of his own caste-men ! In the Cabinet, he always opposed any proposal to commend my work or place me in a position of vantage. I was posted in charge of the C.I.D. (Criminal Investigation Wing) but this could be effected when his prestige ran low consequent on disclosures regarding his illegal gains.

The organisation of B.M.P. battalions was interesting. While a central committee had recommended that there should be an officer of the rank of Deputy S.P. in charge of each company, the government of Bihar would not sanction anything above a half baked, semi literate Subedar. Similar was the case with the other positions. The transport and other equipments were below par. No wonder that this force could not prove as effective as it should have been.

The position in the Home Guards, was much the same. Expansion took place in this force much on the lines of the B.M.P. When a new batch of trainees had to be taken in, it was the regular practice for political groups to push in their own nominees. Though ostensibly for civil defence work and generally to act as police auxiliaries, it was realised that it was a good way of subsidising political fellow travellers. Therefore a case was always made out for employing the largest fraction of these people in duties for which they could get allowances. Even the poor allowances admissible were quite attractive for the men in the countryside—that made the spectacle pathetic. Yet there was no attempt to improve on the training etc. of Home Guards. Their training centre was located in condemned hutments of the erstwhile emergency air-strip at Bihta near Patna, which was put up during the last world war. These hutments kept on tumbling down specially during rains but there was no reaction in the dovecotes of the political leadership. The finance department would put obstacles in the way of fiscal sanctions specially as the group in charge of this organisation was not in full accord with the Finance Minister's group. Whenever there was an incumbent of the same group, things were entirely different. Whenever the passing-out parade of a group of trainees came off, the spectators were mainly of the group of the minister in charge. And the trainees had to cheer him before the function ended. This was resented by some of the stipendiary staff, who were ranged in the other group. The result was that a series of cases of misconduct of one group, testified to by the other, and vice versa cropped up. A Subedar belonging to the group of an ex-C.M., who had arranged for his rapid advancement entered into a lengthy litigation with government. Another Commandant was arraigned for corrupt practices and was later on discharged from service but not before considerable acrimony had been built up between groups in the Home Guards organisation, ranged against each other and bolstered up by the politicians of the two warring factions. This imposed strains unknown to me in the past and interestingly I was labelled as a protege of the Rajput faction, which was indeed absurd and highly slanderous but nothing could be done about it. I suggested setting up a completely separate chain of command for Home Guards or alternatively to scrap the scheme. This did not find favour.

Training of the police force was part of my portfolio. This had been a neglected sector so far. It was fantastic that the centre for giving refresher courses to police investigators, was tagged on to the C.I.D. as the officer there wished to have a share of the kudos. In the State there was only one centre for training Sub-Inspectors located at Hazaribagh, while the constables were trained at Bhagalpur. The training courses had been devised in the pre-independence period and were carried forward blindly. I could hardly have the time to attend to these centres except pay a casual visit, which was thoroughly inadequate. During the war years, the British administrators had placed a retired I.G. as the head of the institution at Hazaribagh. This was pooh poohed by the new dispensation. The only item that interested the political leaders and the police top brass was the annual function at the Police Training College which was now presided over by the Chief Minister. This provided an opportunity to curry favour with this dignitary. As for the Chief Minister, it appeared that he too wished to have personal contact with the Sub-Inspectors, who were likely to be useful once they got into the field of their operations. The Sub Inspector trainees belonging to the C.M's caste made much of the occasion and special loyalties were pledged in private gatherings even though the oath taking on the occasion of the passing-out parade was merely relating to the law and the Constitution. Contrary to earlier practice when the S.Is were appointed under orders of the I.G., the appointment certificate being issued by the Deputy I.G., the C.M. now approved of this. The idea obviously was to ensure that the proteges of the appropriate group got into this service. As noted earlier the C.M. presided over the passing out function regularly and this was done in the past by the I.G.

This considerably denigrated the Inspector General and introduced schisms in the force. In regard to the military police the training procedures were indeed peculiar. While this force was to aid the civil police, they were trained in field tactics, section in attack, digging in etc. as if they were army territorials. At one of the training functions, one of the jawans pompously stated that when faced with the enemy, he would finish each one of them. This expression of devotion to duty was greatly appreciated! This to me provided the lighter side of my chores in these camps.

The Military Police had a mounted unit. Earlier whalers were taken on, but for nearly two decades the local breed was all that was available. The horses had to be purchased from Delhi—I believe the contractor, an M.P., used to get the horses surreptitiously from the stud farms in Pakistan. Sometimes a few could be picked up from fairs in Amritsar and Meerut but the source of supply was the same as horse breeding in India had come nearly to a dead stop. The Indian army was discarding horses and now bore mule units for the mountain divisions. These mules were bred in the country. I wanted a farm to be set up in Bihar to cater not only for the requirements of the state but also for other places. The project remained on paper. In the mounted unit at Arrah, headquarters of the district of Shahabad where the 1857 mutiny had its echoes in Bihar, the spectacle was that of confrontation between the Jat incumbents from East Punjab (now Haryana) and the local Sawars. The incumbents from the Haryana area, sought my support for getting their due. It was impossible to take up all their cases. Though their claims were just and proper, these were not allowed : the result was that most of these incumbents retired and went home. The mounted unit was a poor force now. Previously their performance at police tattoos used to be greatly appreciated. Now it was a job to rig up a few items for these shows. This unit had in the pre-independence period a very large component of burly Pathans, who were first class riders, but these Pathans had all migrated to Pakistan in 1947.

The integration of armed police personnel under one command had still not been achieved, much as it would help improve efficiency. However, the job that I then performed is now the charge of three officers of the rank of Inspector General although there is not much change in the numerical strength of this force. So much for Parkinson's Law.

During my tenure in this post, I visited one of our units loaned to the Tripura administration. While the B.M.P. appeared to have done a good job, the men were generally very unhappy to be there and it was difficult to find the officers to head them. Whoever got selected succeeded in obtaining medical certificates or showed other disabilities. It was therefore a happy day when the unit was withdrawn due to extra requirements of routine work in the state.

A fully organised welfare set-up for the armed constabulary was an urgent requirement. The army, navy and the air force had organisations of this nature and these also assisted the retired personnel in getting job placements in view of their going off the pay-rolls at a comparatively younger age. In the police all that could be arranged was a canteen at some centres working on a no-profit no-loss basis with some staff and accommodation assistance from government. Interestingly enough these canteens changed names with the change in the incumbent of senior posts. When the senior officer retired, the officers running the canteen made haste to rechristen the canteen to get some personal favours from the new officers. In order to get the welfare work going, I pleaded for a share of the collections on the Armed Forces Day which went to the three fighting forces. My argument was that a separate collection for the police may attract unfavourable public comment, specially in view of their poor image. Such collection was allowed for the fire services also. However, the suggestion was vetoed by the Rajyapal himself and he jocularly stated that the police knew how to look after themselves and needed no outside assistance.

11

STATE COALITIONS

AFTER ABOUT twenty years of independence the country faced the periodical general election in 1967. These elections were in many ways a water-shed in the political history of the country as it was the first occasion when parties other than the Congress managed to secure large majorities in some of the state legislatures. And even in the central sphere, the Congress majority was reduced to a very large extent. The result of this exercise was a Samyukt Vidhayak Dal government in Bihar. And with it came a new ministry headed by an ex-Congressman, and an ex-President of the state Congress Committee, who had now become an ardent opponent of the party. Mahamaya Prasad Sinha felt that the Congress had outlived its usefulness. The people in general were also greatly disillusioned with the performance in government of those who had perhaps made sacrifices for the country's independence. These were the very people who, soon after the liberation set about unabashedly lining their own pockets. The so-called freedom fighters were given large pensions and employment benefits which far outstripped the losses that they may have incurred. If any thing kept the common voter from throwing out the old set, it was the appeal to local patriotism, clannishness and casteism. There was a constable in the C.I.D. who stated that he had gone to jail for a few days in 1942 and he now got a pension which exceeded the salary that he earned in his substantive post of constable. This was a good case but a very large number obtained payment for imaginary service established by reference to doubtful witnesses drawn from political supporters. Senior politicians obtained a share of this loot.

The elections made interesting revelations. The first organised effort at "booth capture" came to notice. According to this system voters, who were expected to vote against the party candidate, were desisted from going to the polling booth and the franchise was exercised by bogus means. They were even given a small subsidy to keep away from voting. A favourable Presiding Officer, could also manage to have the voting papers appropriately cast. The demand now was for the ballot box to be carried to the villages and mohallas in towns for collecting the poll papers rather than make the voter come to the booth. This was rejected as impracticable so was the case for making voting compulsory and based on individual identity cards.

In the city of Patna itself responsible persons on going to the booth found that their votes had already been polled. One senior police officer at headquarters, who was living in the official New Patna residential complex, found to this chagrin, when he landed up with his family for casting vote, that this had already been done. He was a Muslim and this was a specially sore point for his correligionists. The number of such cases was very large indeed. A very large number of people were even excluded from the poll list. These revelations had repercussions in the police as well as the police had been integrated with the election process.

One of the ministers lost in the poll. He had objected to police patrol in the neighbourhood of the booths as he thought this would foil his booth capturing plan. The officer in-charge of the patrol, a subordinate magistrate, was threatened with dire consequences by the candidate. It was lucky that the minister lost in the contest and he could not vent his spleen against the magistrate. He settled scores when in the next election he got elected and obtained a place in the state cabinet as well!

The police was always a part of the portfolio of the Chief Minister not only in Bihar but in most of the states in the country. The position was now changed. A new Police Minister came into the picture and this pattern was adopted in other states as well. The intention was to have one person look to all police problems but contrary to the expectation, police work was divided up. The normal operations including that of investigation of cases remained with the Police Minister while the Chief Minister kept to himself the special wing of the police dealing with intelligence and allied matters. This included items like arrests etc., under the Preventive Detention Act for hoarding and smuggling. The police auxiliary, the Home Guards, was also placed under a different minister. There were Ministers of State to boot : result—confusion prevailed in police functioning, quite unknown in the past. One example of this was the release of some persons detained on alleged charge of smuggling and profiteering. This took place without the Police Minister being aware of it. In fact all this was effected by pulling the wire in the C.M.'s personal establishment, which assumed the hues of a scandal. The Police Minister objected to their release, which were made without consulting him and a battle royal ensued. The crisis was heightened as the government consisted of disparate groups of politicians who had merely come together to form a ministry. It was such incidents which led to the undoing of the ministry later. All this did positive harm to the functioning of the police department, some officers swearing allegiance to the Chief Minister while others went with the Police Minister.

The new ministry came up on the crest of popular indignation against the doings of the earlier dispensation. A large fraction of the youth had sided the new leaders and they were so exuberant in their support that even the initial victory celebrations became tumultuous, resulting in some loss of public and private property. The Chief Minister addressed the youth as "a small parcel of his own heart" (*lakht-e-jigar*) and shed tears over their troubles which he knew it would not be possible for him to ameliorate in the short span of his tenure in office. The job of keeping order in meetings addressed by cabinet members became a major hazard for the police as they were not allowed to keep the crowd under control and yet the leaders would have liked the arrangements to be perfectly orderly. On many an occasion the Chief Minister was surrounded and was literally carried off his feet by the milling crowds. The police including the senior officers, mute spectators of this drama, could get a good chit neither from the people nor from the VIPs themselves.

The new Police Minister was a member of the state constabulary and left the force in 1942. According to him he had resigned but the official record showed that he had been proceeded against in a departmental enquiry for indiscipline and misconduct and had been dismissed. This was not an isolated case : there were quite a few such cases. The dismissed constables had followed up by fomenting anti-government agitation among the constabulary. A police rebellion occurred in 1946 and in 1947 as well before independence came. These erstwhile followers were round the Police

Minister and he was being led by them in matters of which they did not have a full knowledge. Senior officers now started conveying their personal grievances and difficulties to the Police Minister through these subordinates who may even have worked under them. Thus a complete confusion in the day-to-day working of the department came up : Police discipline and efficiency was completely gone.

There was in-fighting in the ministry, and this specially affected the police which was used to carry out orders along a single channel of command. The Congress party, when in power, had continued this, but the position now was of various voices guiding the police. Add to it the inexperience of the new members of the cabinet. Ill-informed criticism was hurled on police officers of various ranks including the Inspector General. As Deputy Inspector General in charge of the Criminal Investigation Department I was witness to many a battle between the stalwarts !

The doings of the new ministers were indeed interesting. On receiving a file with a note, "Please see the note placed below," the minister was pleased to comment that he had hunted through the file but could find no note in it. He also recorded that no notes (currency notes?) need be placed in files as this signified blatant corruption! But it was an open secret that orders could be obtained from even the Chief Minister with an appropriate contact with his brother who ran his household. The brother had a run of the official files and records. Such contact men were round all ministers. Thus corruption had a finesse unknown in the past. It was all a question of the various contact men settling the deals and the ministers were but mute participants. A comment which was generally made was that the predecessor government consisted of the lot who had satiated themselves, but the new set needed some time to fill their bellies. It was only the Communist bloc which presented a general picture of honesty though the black sheep were visible in this set as well. The S.V.D. government did not last long and after a few months yielded place to another, whereafter there was a succession of short term ministries. All this caused not a little amusement all round. The common comment was relating to *ayaram* and *gyaram*, members of the legislature crossing the floor and resulting in the ministries being toppled. Some of the ministries lasted for a few days only. All this happened not as a result of any ideological considerations but on purely personal or parochial grounds. The most important casualty in all this was the morale of the police, the armed guards for a minister moving from house to house every few days and witnessing the funny drama being staged. It became customary now for senior police officers to make a daily routine of going to the political camps to feel the pulse of the legislators. They had to jockey for position to keep firm in the saddle or else they would be bundled off from one position to another during the course of a few days only. There were a very large number of cases in which postings and transfers of senior police personnel followed no principles whatsoever. The C.I.D. (intelligence wing) reports were quite often bandied about in public, leaking out from the seats of power. Every new ministry would also stall the orders passed by the earlier regime and that made confusion worse confounded.

There were several spells of Presidential rule when for a brief period the administration worked under the guidance of the Rajyapal but in fact it meant a period of complete stagnation when nothing was done. The interim governments could not take any decision worth the name. Then in 1969 came the sundering of the giant Congress party into two organizations, and with it there was another unit added to the likely permutation and combination for ministry formation. Confusion was worse confounded.

One of the chief ministers of the period—Bhola Shastri, was assured of full support in the house by his group but when the day's proceedings started, he found that the tables had been turned against him. The Raja of Ramgarh's group wanted favourable orders to be passed in their case which the C.M. had found difficult to accede to. The Chief Minister decided to remain in his own chamber listening to the debate on the floor of the House through the speaker fitted in his room and did not enter the hall at all. He quietly proceeded to the Raj Bhawan, and tendered his resignation. This volte face in the members of the legislature was quite common signifying absence of loyalties and erosion in the values of democracy.

There was an interesting case at this time in which a saree was reportedly stolen from a box in the residential section of the Raj Bhavan occupied by the Rajyapal's family. This saree was earlier purchased from a local shop. The investigation did not cut much ice but I was happy to learn a few days later that the stolen saree was recovered from the bushes near Raj Bhavan staff quarters. One of the members of the Raj Bhavan staff was alleged to have pointed out in the bushes on the fringe of the Raj Bhavan a broken down package and it contained the stolen saree. I knew that the saree which was stolen did not carry a blouse piece. However, I learnt later that the recovered saree did have the blouse pieec with it. I did not like to pursue enquiries as the matter was old and the investigation could not yield any substantial material for action. Obviously the local shop had a duplicate of the stolen saree available : a new trend in police investigation technique !

There was considerable emphasis on anti-smuggling measures, because of a shortfall in food production throughout the country. This was specially so in Bihar. The problem was accentuated due to the absence of any sizable buffer stock in the state, belonging to the State or the Government of India. There was need to establish special cordons in each state to ensure that the foodgrains produced in the state were not taken out surreptitiously to other states while the local people languished for it. In West Bengal a fairly large force was rigged up for this work, but in Bihar the police in the field were saddled with these duties. In the central sphere, the Government of India had set up a special cell in the Central Bureau of Investigation to coordinate such state activities. Against this backdrop the State Chief Minister B.P. Mandal, later to be appointed Chairman of the Backward Classes Commission of the Government of India in 1978, whose ministry lasted for barely two months, called a meeting of senior police officers and also of the Department of Supply. He ordered that a scheme be prepared forthwith for the setting up of a police unit composed of policemen and Home Guards and officered by an Inspector General of Police of the state cadre. A proposal was prepared by me at his behest but the Chief Secretary raised objections to this being done. The Finance Department had their own point of view. In spite of clear orders, this scheme was so enmeshed in departmental red tape that the C.M. felt completely frustrated and nothing was done. The abject helplessness of the Chief Minister, who was Head of the State administration, in enforcing a measure which was considered absolutely necessary by the State Cabinet, was a signal of the inefficiency and ineptitude of the administration. It showed that it was really the bureaucracy which mattered. I had to prepare the scheme as ordered by the Chief Minister and after he had laid down office, I was informed that I should not have prepared such a scheme. Apparently the scheme as prepared did not fit into the power pattern of the state ; and senior police officers were wanting to sabotage it as well as it would mean advancement for some who did not belong to their group.

The question came up about this time of the supply of rum to Gurkha armed constables, who had been provided this during the winter months as they were required to perform arduous duties in chilly weather. This was the style which had been followed in the army as well and the military police had merely borrowed this system from them. The rum was obtained from the manufacturing units near Asansol in West Bengal and the excise on it was forgone by the government to enable the supplies to be made at reasonable rates. The market rates for retail sale were too high for the poorly paid constables. A very high powered meeting was called by the Excise Minister who incidentally was well known for his fondness for the bottle. As required by the country's Constitution, it was decided that alcoholic drinks should not be provided to the constabulary and they should buy their drinks from the open market. The Gurkhas promptly reacted and even claimed the drinks, which they said had the support of religious usage. Finally the orders were set aside by the government in relation to Gurkhas. In their case, the approved ration included a dose of rum. Apparently all decisions were taken in half hearted way and there was no desire to ensure compliance. "Order for order's sake" was the new thesis.

The advisers' regimes declaring themselves as caretakers under the superintendence of the state Rajyapal, virtually turned out to be a machine for helping members of the Indian Administrative Service. The jobs of the rank of Commissioner were multiplied overnight and each Secretary to the Government department was raised to the rank of Commissioner. The question asked was if the Secretariat could now be termed as Commissioneriat. For the police, it meant a back slide as no extra jobs were sanctioned on the senior level. A retired police officer was considered for posting as adviser but it fell through due to the opposition of the administrative service officers. The post of I.G., as also of the Chief Secretary, was so far of the rank of Commissioner. Now the Chief Secretary was raised one level in scale by being made equivalent to the Additional Secretary to the Government of India, while the I.G. Police, the only one in the state, was bracketed with Commissioners, whose number was legion. The police department as a whole lost face in this process and their chief was denigrated considerably. Incidentally the Chief Secretary has since been raised to the status of a Secretary to the Government of India ministries.

On each occasion of a change in the government including the switch over to the rule of the advisers, it appeared that the police chief would be a casualty. In almost all States, each change in the ministry, even if it meant a change in the Chief Minister only, the party in power being the same, the I.G. of Police was always changed. On many an occasion the discarded officer was given an honorific title and was kept on the shelf, with no work. In some cases even a raise in the badges of rank was given, though it meant keeping him away from the normal police work. Therefore the principal item of discussion in police forums was not the question of improvement in procedures, rules, or standards of work, but merely the question of postings, and promotions. It was openly stated that large sums of money changed hands to acquire positions of vantage in which favours could be doled out. Simultaneously the Indian Police Service was getting more and more under the wings of the central government. The frequent imposition of President's rule was another factor which contributed to all this. All senior appointments now appeared to be decided at the level of the Government of India, and were not the I.A.S. and I.P.S. centrally controlled services ? This had no administrative or constitutional justification, but this was the way the problem was tackled.

An alarming aspect of these developments was the atmosphere of conspiracy engendered in the department. The additional I.G. formed a gang of some of the senior officers, whom he got around on caste and other not too complimentary considerations. A tirade was started against the chief designating him as a nincompoop and a broken down horse fit for the destruction line. It was easy for this set to pull in some political elements as well with which the government could be pressurised. The facilities of the Special Branch were freely utilised in furtherance of this plan. Whispering campaigns were started and the central government officials like the Central Intelligence officer as also second line central legislators were pulled in to cause greater confusion. The sight was reminiscent of the days of Pathan rule in the country during the early years of their ascendancy during the regime of Razia Sultana. The plans of this coterie aimed at expanding the top ranks in the police with a view to getting early promotion and in this game the scruples were not many. Cases of corruption and nepotism were slurred over and also criminals—smugglers and black markeeters—could get protection. All this did bring about a breakdown in the health of the I.G., which added to the arguments of this disgruntled camp. The third force had no place in this game and I felt unhappy that nothing could be done to stem the rot. The police were indeed going down an avalanche.

An interesting development was the setting up of coordination committees of the political parties sharing power in the state so as to control the working of government. These coordination committees appeared to act as super cabinets examining all cabinet decisions and even forestalling them at times by taking decisions which had to be implemented by the government. The proceedings of these coordination committee meetings were widely publicised and indicated the trend. The police force had now to tolerate interference in the maintenance of law and order and even in investigation of crimes by these polyglot bodies.

The state of discipline in the police force is well exemplified in the incident noted below. The C.I.D. of which I was in charge had several superintendents dealing with functional matters ; one of these officers, a son-in-law of a minister and a close associate of the C.M. came up to me one day after his annual confidential report had been written up. I remembered to have recorded that his work was of fair quality. This officer had, however, got used to encomiums being recorded in his roll because of his political connections. Though a confidential record, my remarks were promptly passed on to him by no less a person that the Inspector General himself. This officer, otherwise very well behaved, appeared to behave awkwardly when he came to me on this occasion. He candidly stated that the I.G. had informed him about my remarks, which were not to his liking. He wanted to know what had merited these remarks. I had to tell him off for his peculiar behaviour. The normal process was for the gist of unfavourable remarks to be passed on to the concerned officers under government orders. It was clear that these remarks would not fall in this category and would not have been conveyed to him but for the I.G.'s anxiety to seek favours of the coterie to which this S.P. belonged. Confidential marking on official papers had lost all significance and these leaked out from the very sectors, which were supposed to preserve their secrecy.

Another incident which may interest related to a head constable. I was on a visit to Dhanbad and was proceeding along to the Circuit House, in the car of a friend—an honorary magistrate and a mine owner. The honorary magistrate was at the wheel. A level crossing bisected Dhanbad township. It remained notoriously closed for long periods. On this occasion, the level crossing was open, and that was lucky but two policemen including one head constable in shabby uniform, stopped the car peremptorily and asked for a ride. The magistrate, informed them that he was in a hurry and had a friend with him, pointing towards me, but the policemen, undeterred, got into the car and forced the magistrate to take them towards their post of duty. They had the good sense of informing the honorary magistrate that they were coming after their lunch for which they never made any payment to the local restaurant. They also reported that they had to leave their post of duty rather irregularly and so were in a hurry. The car was taken by the honorary magistrate first to the Circuit House where I had to go and it is here the head constable realised what had happened as the armed guard turned out to pay compliments to me. The policemen were suspended and were later dismissed from service. The incident leaked out to press via the honorary magistrate and attracted interesting headlines in the press in the country. One so far as I remember, said—"A free ride to suspension". The incident showed the great decline in standards of police work and their respect for authority.

The plethora of inexperienced and ill educated ministers resulted in a sad exhibition on the occasion of the police parade. The Home Minister, who was to board the jeep for inspecting the parade, was promptly followed by the Minister of State for Police as well who had to be physically removed from the scene to avoid his standing in the jeep alongside the Home Minister to receive a joint salute of the parading policemen ! In the exuberance of his newly acquired authority this Minister of State would visit police stations and wanted to inspect records which were strictly for departmental check. He wanted to see investigation records of cases in which his friends were involved. As the police officer refused to show his record, he was threatened with dire consequences. It took some arguments on my part to convince the Home Minister also that the Minister of State had acted improperly.

The lack of respect for rules erupted as acts of indiscipline by students. There were unsavoury scenes on educational campuses. The police were unable to control the situation, as they were ill trained to act in such situations and various restrictions had also been placed on their activities in these areas. There was a recrudesence of communal trouble also. Sectarian groups staged communal incidents to wreak vengeance on their enemies or even embarrass the ruling group in the government. During one of the terms of the Samyukt Vidhayak Dal government of Bihar, there was an outbreak of serious communal trouble in Ranchi. Unable to control the situation the district administration handed over charge to the army authorities. It was a moot question if this could be effected by local officers and if it meant handing over completely to the army. This delayed the effective action to restore normalcy. To add to it, the Home Minister of the State became extremely active and wished to assume control of the operations for which he did not have the requisite capability. His experience in this work was that of a constable. The local police were hard put to protect his person, leave aside providing general protection to the populace in the area.

Chief Minister Karpuri Thakur's style of functioning, came up for a lot of criticism particularly in regard to his personal security. One fine morning it was flashed in the press that a large group of disgruntled partymen had invaded the Chief Minister's residence at night, broken down the gate, bypassed the security sentry and had effected entrance into his bedroom. The Chief Minister would not allow any force whatsoever to be used and held a long discussion with the intruding political workers right in his own bedroom. The broken down gate of the C.M's residence remained unrepaired for a long time, a mute spectator of the confusion that was the working of the political system in the state. The Chief Minister now adopted the style of the Mansabdars of the Mughal days by moving from place to place each night and even his partymen were kept guessing about where he could be found. On one such occasion he spent the night in a station wagon alongside the highway bypass near the capital. His only companion on this occasion was his personal police guard. On another occasion he retired to the house of a senior civil servant, a bachelor, and remained there for three days to dispose of files which he carted about in a police pick-up van. The police was engaged in a shadow play and had no effective role in security matters.

12

POLICE CHIEF

IN THE midst of all this confusing scene, I was successively promoted as Additional Inspector General and later as Inspector General of the state. This was effected as I was the seniormost incumbent in the Indian police cadre in the state and though a no-party man, I could be bypassed only at the risk of serious public criticism. On each occasion of the promotion, it appeared that special jobs would be found for me but somehow this did not happen. Even under the Government of India the position was the same and all appointments of this nature had similar manoeuvres tagged on. Fate was now the most important factor. It was not as if an officer got his due but as if the politicians resigned to this alternative when they did not have any other options open. The post of I.G. had been completely kneaded in the political cauldron. A post of prestige, enjoying final authority in several matters and with a say in all matters of importance, now the incumbent had to play to the tune of those in power. If he failed to act accordingly, his future in the department was sealed. The earlier Congress government in the state functioning under the wings of Delhi, had earned notoriety by throwing aside more than a dozen capable officers of the I.C.S. and I.A.S., later to be elevated to much higher posts in favour of a junior promotee from the provincial civil service to fill up the post of chief secretary. Some such development could have taken place in the police as well, but the Congress government fell under the dead weight of its own acts of omission and commission and had given place to a multiparty government that took the decision in my favour. The various constituents of the new government were credited with considerable horse trading in filling up important posts. But the

Home Minister, who had functioned in the earlier S.V.D. governments as such, was now installed in the same capacity. He was chastened by his earlier experience, and would not brook any interference in the working of the departments under him. He prepared the proposal for my appointment while on a flight to Jamshedpur in a state government plane. He showed the papers only to a few trusted friends so that no opposition could be organised in the cabinet. He also saw to it that his group was present in full strength in the cabinet meeting where this item was discussed. I was candidly told all this by the Home Minister himself after the proposal was through. He was the first to telephone me about this decision.

The Inspector General of Police in the earlier regime could make postings of all officers of the rank of Deputy Superintendent of Police and posting of higher ranks had to be under government orders which was a mere formality as it was the Inspector General who had to decide about the appropriateness of the positions. The position was a complete reversal now. The Inspector General would learn about orders of postings of his subordinates through the local papers. The atmosphere was reminiscent of the years of decadence of the Mughal rule.

A proposal was sent by me for transfer of some Deputy Superintendents of police. This involved the posting of a "non controversial" officer at Hajipur. But the stormy Rajput zamindars of the area wanted an officer of their own caste. The Home Minister was impressed and ordered this posting though the recommendation was entirely different. The other group had the support of the Chief Minister and so the Chief Minister wanted me to change the orders, little realising that the orders were passed by his colleague, the Home Minister. He accused me of supporting Rajput officers while the fact was that my recommendations were different. He would not ask the Home Minister about it directly. There was a battle of wits between the two senior ministers over this petty matter, each accusing the other of acting under the influence of some caste-ist leaders. On one occasion this difference escalated into open accusations between the two in my presence. I was happy that the Chief Minister realised then that I had made no parochial proposals and that the only solution to such questions was to remove these postings from the aegis of the political bosses. Such matters should be decided by the police chief, who is responsible to the government for its efficient functioning. But this was not to be.

The Minister of State for Home Affairs went on a visit to a police station in distant Giridih sub-division. He did not find the local sub-inspector there. The minister sent for the head constable and gave vent to his spleen against the sub-inspector as the latter had not been fair to a relation of the minister. This relation did not possess too good a reputation. Not content, however this minister declared that the S.I. was transferred. The question of the sub-inspector's misconduct had been thoroughly investigated and he had been ordered to continue at his post of duty. The minister, however, insisted on the S.I. moving away at once, and finding no response he declared the officer suspended! But such orders required formal ratification. The connected papers, therefore, came to the police headquarters later with notes of the intermediate officers all in favour of the S.I. A battle royal ensued as the minister's orders were entirely wrong and not enforceable. The minister even threatened to rig up a cabinet crisis. Luckily the ministry surrendered office then and the storm blew over. But it left its scars on the morale of the subordinate police officers. The Home Minister had supported the official stand and consequently the two ministers had ceased to be on talking terms ! The Government of India in the Home Ministry had appointed a committee of senior police officers in the country under my chairmanship to formulate a standard code for the functioning of the State Criminal Investigation Departments. I was then the Additional Inspector General of the state. I had to go to various states to finalise this report. An officer of the C.B.I., John Lobo, later to become the Director of the organization, was its Secretary. We found the position in all the states practically the same with scant consideration for the lot of the police and no attempt at improving investigation techniques. We prepared a comprehensive report which I believe adorns the archives of each state and nothing worth the name was done. I felt unhappy at the way the matter was proceeding in the country and hoped that on taking over charge as I.G. I would take up the matter strongly so that the police were not neglected. I also intended to rid the force of its internal schisms and social stratification in ranks which had marred its usefulness. Before assuming charge of my new duties as the police chief, I could also make a tour of Europe, America, and East Asia. I visited the Interpol which had its headquarters at Paris. This organization showed how effective international cooperation in crime prevention was possible despite political barriers: in fact this was the only international organisation which was working outside the ambit of the U.N. India needed a mini-Interpol of her own because of the larger and varied terrain covered. At Washington, I visited the academy for training of the police, the facilities of which were availed of by various other countries as well, particularly in the developing sector. The systems engendered by the academy were working very effectively. I was full of these ideas when I took over command of the state police. But to begin with I was occupied fully with general elections for the Lok Sabha which were held a year in advance of the schedule. Mrs. Indira Gandhi wanted to cash in on her popularity following the success in the eastern sector of the sub continent where a new Bangla Desh was carved out. She made a whirlwind tour of the country and the Chhota Nagpur belt of Bihar received her special attention as the sagging morale of her Congress party required a boost. She danced with the tribals on the streets of Ranchi, which enthused them greatly. She addressed the chiefs of the public sector undertakings in south Bihar to provide a new image of her party to the labour and the executives engaged in this sector. She gave the call for *Garibi Hatao*. The fact that the state was under a multiparty government made my task as I.G. Police indeed difficult particularly vis-a-vis Lok Sabha elections. It was likely that the Congress party would come back with a thumping majority at the centre but in the state the picture would be different, as there were going to be no elections at this time for the state Vidhan Sabha. However, even the state Home Minister gleefully asserted during the elections that Indiraji would sweep the polls. He was a Brahmin by caste and had reasons to be happy over such a contingency. I had some information that overtures had been made by the Congress party to win him over to their side. The more interesting matter was the request made to me by Congress candidates in the elections asking for the posting of certain officers including Station House Officers in their constituencies. The supporters of the state government were naturally opposed to all this. These postings would have been a complete negation of the accepted rules of conducting the elections as there was a complete moratorium on transfers on election eve. Yet the Congress candidates would spit fire and venom in support of their unreasonable request, justifying it by some imaginary precedents.

We were faced at this time with the violent movement led by a section of the Communist party (Marxist Leninist). They placed their faith in the old methods adopted by the terrorists of the British regime. Their thesis was that Indian society was being riven, as during the British regime, into the opulent few and the poor masses ; the latter were unable to make a dent in the problem of their poverty unless they adopted shock tactics. Therefore, a few usurious money lenders and *Seths* in the countryside and some of the minions of the law, who were apparently supporting the capitalist structure, had to be silenced. This was done in as cruel a manner as possible so as to act as a deterrent to others. According to the agitators a movement such as this was likely to result in chaos in the ranks of the money-bags who had no morale to withstand such onslaughts. Therefore unwary policemen moving in the countryside were surprised and hacked to death. Some armed guards were attacked and their rifles and ammunition were looted to provide the weapons for future attacks. Such incidents focused attention of the people towards the inefficiency and lack of alertness of the law keepers, who were the pride of the state. These terrorists were given the name of Naxalites deriving the nomenclature from Naxalbari in West Bengal. They created a reign of terror in Bengal, Bihar, Orissa, and Andhra Pradesh. In regard to police work, I framed special orders, laying down the security precautions to be taken. The rifles were ordered to be secured to the body of the constable so that snatching it unawares would not be possible. In case of a murderous assault, the dead body of the policeman had to be carried some distance before the rifle could be removed. Special protection had to be given to lone policemen doing traffic control and other duties and some watch groups were earmarked to be stationed at hand with spears. This had an obvious impact on the police force in the eastern part of the country and made the constables more alert. The text of the order issued was leaked out by some officer of the state intelligence to the Hindi periodical *Din Man*. While this did indicate to the Naxalites our resolve to contain and oppose them in their spree of violence, it failed to help the disgruntled intelligence officers as the state government felt gratified that the police chief had taken preventive measures in advance. They were all in agreement with what was being done. The perfidy to which the intelligence organisation was set was obvious and this mirrored the difference in the government itself. Yet it was astounding how this creaky administration could go forward, the Chief Secretary pulling with the disgruntled wing of the police and perhaps having the blessing of the Chief Minister. The Home Minister and the Chief did not see eye to eye with each other either.

The Chief Secretary—the post was now equated with a Secretary to the Government of India—was a member of the state civil service and had been promoted as mentioned earlier to this post over the head of about a dozen senior officers. There was a writ petition moved in the High Court at Patna against this order. The order of promotion was upheld by the high court and I was told that the superseded officers were intending to move the Supreme Court of India. All this supercession was made by a Congress led government and the ushering in of a United Front government which had placed me in position was expected to result in upsetting of this key appointment as well. But this Chief Secretary, being a member of the backward classes, had a point in his favour. The new cabinet was riven into groups based on the backward and forward castes. The position of the Chief Secretary became therefore doubly secure. The Chief Minister, openly expressed his gratification at the judgement of the High Court and let things go on.

A continuation of the Naxalite agitation was the attempt at jail break by the detenus particularly from the central jails at Patna and Hazaribagh. Some Naxalites and a few hardened dacoits could succeed in their attempt. This focused attention on the thoroughly inefficient and corrupt prison administration. It was found that old fangled leg chains and fetters were used for the detenus, but these proved ineffective. The large scale pointless firing resorted to by the jail warders was another point which was mooted in the press and even in the houses of the legislature. Prison and police reforms had to go hand in hand. The Naxalite agitation brought this to the fore but only in a very ephemerals way. I visited the affected jails with the Chief Minister. Apart from pious resolutions, nothing appeared to materialise. The conditions in the jails continued to be apalling and a disgrace to the administration.

The Chief Minister could make an air dash to these centres but it really meant nothing at all.

The new dispensation under the united front banner was anxious to streamline the police force but felt helpless in a way due to their own internal differences. They appointed a commitee to revise the police regulations, which would be the harbinger of re-structuring the entire police force also. However, this committee could hardly function as coming close on the heels of the victory of the Congress at the polls, internal differences in the united front came to the surface and the government fell. And with this went the newly constituted committee as well Earlier the government had appointed a committee of the legislature to revise the state police manual, which as an item of minor legislation fell within its purview. This was also to fulfil an assurance given on the floor of the house. Successive meetings of this body could not make much progress as the accent was on getting out on a travel spree to study the position in different localities. Many of the members of this committee became ministers in the state cabinet in one government or another and the strength of the committee was decimated. The discussions in these committee meetings therefore proceeded slower than was anticipated. A short report was prepared but this was not adequate. Therefore the new committee was set up, but it was still born. Speaking about reforms in the police, the state government under the Congress party had appointed a Commission in 1958—other states had also done this—which provided employment to retired sycophants. The Commission made recommendations after nearly three years of labour, all of which were found not practical and were shelved. It was in view of this that the Committee had been set up but it fell a prey to the political clime in the state.

There was a succession of short term ministries in the state some of which were headed by groups having the support of the Congress party. In the last elections in the state the Congress party had not done too well and the schism in the Congress had further weakened this group. This was a prelude to state elections as well. One could only watch and see the fortunes of local leaders which indicated political hobnobbing at the central level of the Congress party. It was now stated in the press that state autonomy notwithstanding, a strong government at the centre should make an effective impression on the set up in the state.

In regard to the police department the invisible hand of the central Home Ministry veered the fortunes of senior police officers even more blatantly. It was again the same question of dual loyalties. How could this hiatus in loyalty be solved ? There was renewed demand from some states for the abolition of the centrally controlled all-India services. This demand was particularly loud and vociferous from West Bengal and some of the southern states. All this affected the morale and the standard of work of the apex service. The position was not much different for the rank and file in the state. Even in the state, the differences between the Police Minister and the Chief Minister resulted in division of loyalties. The senior officers also lost their credibility as all the good that could be done to subordinates sprang from political manipulation. In the disciplined police force therefore there was a crisis of loyalty and the unity of functioning was completely gone. In the Secretariat, officials held separate conclaves with the police officers of their ilk.

The differences in the political command, had interesting repercussions. In a colliery near Dhanbad, a strike was engineered by a section of the labour union well-disposed towards the Home Minister while the Labour Minister adorned the other camp. Therefore, the Labour Department would castigate the law and order forces for soft pedalling the issue while the Home Department thought that law and order forces should come into the picture in labour disputes only if a violent clash was imminent. It was however, impossible to lay down the line when a law and order situation had developed fully for interference by the police. A circular order issued on the point became the subject of vehement discussion and was designated as purely partisan even by several departments of the government. A labour leader was arrested for inciting violence and the police officer who effected the arrest was promptly suspended under government orders. The senior police officers were helpless and the only alternative for them would have been to lay down office and retire. The junior officers were chagrined and became rebellious or got more and more involved in the local politics, bending over backwards to oblige those who were in positions of vantage.

Political goings on had a bizarre outcrop in the state. As long as Baba Srikrishna Singh remained Chief Minister of the State, Babu Jagjiwan Ram, holding various portfolios at the centre, was for all practical purposes persona-non-grata with the ruling clique. The succession of short term ministries, some of them led by Congress factions depending on Babuji's support made his influence felt in the state sphere as well though each time an election took place it was stated that he had every possibility of losing in the fray. This, however, never came off. For once Babuji's only son Suresh was to be inducted in the state ministry yet the local pulls did not allow this to come through. His *Samdhin*, Mrs Sumitra Devi was a minister in the state on more than one occasion. As a policeman I had several occasions to be near Babuji. Always careful not to intrude on the sphere of work of stipendiary staff, he at times made recommendations for the transfer of officers in his constituency though often these could not be complied with. Naturally these were not straight forward cases of applying the rules or else no *pairvi* was necessary. The request made by him during the tenure of a non-Congress ministry had difficult sailing, and could not be complied with. This was all a case of divided loyalties in the junior police formations, who looked for political support rather than the anchor provided by the laws and the police regulations, or the senior police officers.

In regard to the police in the villages, the watch and ward work had been done traditionally by chowkidars who were only part-time government employees. These chowkidars were paid a pittance and had no uniform, training, or discipline. They did not enjoy powers of arrest. They were expected to play to the tune of the subordinate police staff of the police station when on tour in the villages. No action had been taken so far to reform this force or ameliorate their conditions of work. Naturally they were prone to political propaganda and of this there was no dearth with the horde of half baked political workers in the countryside itching to inch forward. The chowkidars mounted an assault on the state Secretariat and attempted to paralyse all work, unless their grievances were redressed. The officials working in the state Secretariat building made their way into their office with great difficulty. Even the ministers found it difficult to break the cordon and attend the state legislature meetings. The ministers would not allow any force to be used for removing the chowkidars who were offering *dharna*. At one stage the surging crowd of chowkidars made its way into the main secretariat building and may have entered the office rooms and the cabinet meeting. This could be avoided with great difficulty. These chowkidars were led by an M.L.A. of the ruling party. This M.L.A. later appeared in the uniform of a chowkidar in my office room to represent the case of the chowkidars. Apparently he had committed a gross illegality by using the uniform of a chowkidar, whatever it was. Yet he was uncontrollable and the incident merely brought a smile on the face of the Chief Minister, whose protege he was. Nothing much could be done except that the arrears of the salary of the chowkidars were paid but it did set the M.L.A. on the path of leadership.

The state of discipline in the department had reached its nadir. In one of the selection boards for promotion of subordinate police officers to higher ranks, one of the D.I.G.s held a brief for a subordinate who did not have a bright record of service. With casteist support, he managed to obtain the favour of some other officers so that in case of voting the worthless officers could get promotion over the head of others. However, finding that this could not be feasible, the D.I.G. quietly slid away from the Board meeting and would not attend its further deliberations. He committed this act of indiscipline with impunity as I was informed he had the support of the Home Minister himself ! Interestingly this D.I.G. was proposed to be given an elevation in rank and minutes were recorded accordingly by the minister. This did not come off as the concerned proposal was not supported by me and in fact was opposed. This caused a considerable flutter in the higher ranks of the bureaucracy and the concerned officer was allowed to gang up a group with the tacit support of ministers so that they could dislodge me to an innocuous post, if possible. The politicians were now feeling surer of their grounds with the rift in the police top brass and felt that interference may not cause upset in the day to day working of the department. To say the least the situation was deplorable.

Cabinet meetings were held on the basis of previously prepared agenda. It appeared, however, that a good deal of decisions were now taken impromptu. The I.G. Police did not have to appear before any of these meetings. One Tuesday evening, however, I was summoned to the meeting of the cabinet. These meetings were held on Tuesdays and full cabinet rank ministers, entitled to attend all meetings, were known as *mangalwari* ministers. Even the refreshments served in these meetings on Tuesdays, were becoming a subject of common talk in the capital as this was in fact a banquet. I did not know why I was sent for, but I realised on arrival that I was to report on the progress of investigation of a case of cheating and embezzlement in which a two-day tenure Chief Minister of yore and some other dignitaries were involved. I declined to disclose the details of investigation but assured them that this work would be duly completed by the special investigators. There was an obvious flutter at my attitude, little realising that it was improper for me to disclose this information. Not content, with this, several cabinet ministers wanted some favourable posting of subordinate police officers to be made to which I reacted by stating that I would take note of the desire of the ministers and issue such orders if these were in accord with the regulations on the point. The pandemonium at the meeting was not a good portent for our democracy. Even though it was known that these ministers had a brief spell to go, and they were themselves aware of it all, they started making claims to big bungalows for their residence, rather than carry on in the two roomed tenement of an M.L A. One of them moved into a big house allotted to him but was dislodged from his position the day he moved in. All these incidents added greatly to the lowering of the people's morale. And with it the police discipline also suffered a severe slump. Senior officers with ephemeral political support of this type, saw several sharp curves in their professional career, adding to the amusement of the people and confusion amongst the subordinate staff.

An important incident which occurred about this time was the surrender of dacoits in the Chambal ravines area. This was done under the wings of Jaya Prakash Narayan who had his headquarters at Patna. One of these dacoits happened to make a visit to Patna on the eve of the surrender to settle the modalities of this event. There was a heavy reward for his capture. Having registered at a local hotel under an assumed name this dacoit had the mortification later on to have his wallet stolen from the hotel room, where he was staying. J.P. suspected that this may have been done by some interested party so as to upset his plan and wanted that enquiries should be so directed without the identity of the dacoit being disclosed. No clue could be found regarding the person who had decamped with the wallet. The surrender of dacoits went on according to plan soon after. The case showed how ineffective investigation work had become. This was specially so after the 1967 polls. What with interference with investigating staff by all and sundry and the engagement of the personnel concerned in other duties. The dacoit Madho Singh even referred to this incident on the passing away of J.P.

An incident which mirrored the state of discipline of the police force and the power it wielded with the politician, was a scene in the premises of the local legislature. A D.I.G. of police, whose family happened to be well known to the then Chief Minister's family, walked into the Chief Minister's chambers and delivered a sermon to him on the appropriateness of certain transfers of police officers ordered by government. The chief minister could not counter the reasonableness of the D.I.G.'s assertion and made no comment then. He, however, made a complaint of it to me suggesting that the D.I.G. may be told to be more polite towards him. The Chief Secretary wanted the D.I.G. to be suspended for indisciplined conduct. However, the D.I.G. made it clear to me that he had talked to the C.M. as an individual known to his family for long and not as a police officer as he could not meet the C.M. without informing me and taking appropriate permission. This was perfectly in order. It was clear that government officers with local support could have a hand in important affairs irrespective of the position held. Non-local officers were but second class citizens.

Earlier there were interesting developments vis-a-vis the movement in Bangladesh, of which certain leaders had come to Patna for support. The assistance to them had to be rightly routed after appropriate checks through the Government of India. The Bangladesh refugees who clustered on the bordering areas in the state also presented a problem of their own, with which the police had to wrestle. We had to mobilise Home Guards to form groups in the border areas to keep vigil over these camps so that trouble may not spread in the countryside. It was impossible to stem the tide of the incoming refugees, and they were all Hindus. Naturally this exacerbated communal feelings. With the Bangladesh leaders, almost all of whom were Muslims, it was a difficult case of keeping the balance. We were informed that the Bihari Muslim immigrants in Bangladesh were more active in their effort to drive away the Hindu element and to appease the nationalist elements. During this period our border forces, which were looking after the incoming refugees, were fusilladed by Pakistani forces and on one occasion some of our senior officers narrowly escaped being hit. I was in the area and some firing took place in our direction. Police function was not only of maintaining internal security but also of protecting the country's frontiers even though this was the charter of the Border Security Force. The chief minister even made a private visit incognito to meet friends in Bangladesh. He gave assistance to some despite the note of caution given by me. It was really a case of "all's well that ends well". He even enlisted the support of Nepali Congress elements in this adventure and this luckily did not misfire. The C.M. who was a Hindi enthusiast, insisted on all the papers coming to him in that language. And he chose to completely ignore notes recorded in English. He received an important letter from the P.M. in English regarding Bangladesh. Although some action on the lines suggested by the P.M. had already been taken in the state, the C.M. quietly filed the letter without taking any action and asked for a Hindi version of this communication.

The general elections of 1971 gave a strong mandate to the Congress and this party started to govern the entire country as if it was one single unit. In regard to the police the story was a repetition of what was happening during the British regime with the difference that a subjective tone was added. Senior police officers even in the middle rungs, depended for their postings on the central government authorities notwithstanding that several states, and Bihar was one, were being governed by United Front ministries. These state ministries were in a state of flux and in the regroupings the Congress party, in power at the centre, got the whip hand in state affairs as well. However, apart from interference which suited the central government, little was done for the police. Schemes for housing of police personnel, long overdue, were financed by the central government, and some amount was earmarked for modernisation of police forces. But this was a drop in the ocean. Each state had the report of its Police Commission and the centre took up the work of coordination ; which implied nothing substantial. The state I.Gs were frequently summoned to the Home Ministry to bring them round to considering the centre as their real fount of authority. Schemes were drawn up to show the state police along the frontier areas ; to engender a sense of belonging to a centralised force. In this they were buttressed by the CRPF and BSF, both of which operated as central police forces. Not content a central committee was set up to consider the problems of police training and recruitment. It produced a valuable report a year later but the problem again was of implementation and the wherewithal for it. The setting up of this committee, however, was the result of a court intrigue in which the Director of the Intelligence Bureau was shunted off to work with the committee. Police officers high and low were expected to knuckle to political authority now. This trend pointed to the development of extra departmental centres of power that presaged the emergency of 1975.

At this stage swearing in ceremonies became very frequent events in the state Raj Bhavan. There were occasions when all ceremonies were arranged with the usual trooping in of the Rajyapal and his aides, but the ministers to be sworn in would not arrive due to some last minute hitch. It was a common joke that cycle rickshaw pullers in town would not make the journey to the Raj Bhavan lest they be invested with the honourable responsibility of a minister in the state cabinet ! The general atmosphere was of unconcern for those who occupied the positions of authority and ministership lost its glamour and prestige.

A large number of agitations particularly amongst students, government employees, and in the labour employed in public sector industries came up. An authoritarian armed police force was unable to tackle them. The idea of converting the police force into a civil police service appeared to be merely a slogan, broadcast from the platforms and in the press. The police were not to enter the temples of learning and yet there were numerous occasions when they were castigated for not interfering and sometimes even for interfering, if this did not suit the arguments of a coterie. In the Patna University the Vice-Chancellor was *gheraoed* by his students for grievances which were apparently peurile. He did not need the assistance of the police, yet he rang up the local police chief and asked him to send a posse of armed policemen under a senior officer. The police force was appropriately sent but the Vice-Chancellor did not let them enter the campus and merely used this device to show himself off before the students. He told them that he could summon the police force as he liked. This V.C. was later severely mauled and manhandled by the students and he had no compunction in handing over the local administration on a gold platter, stating how inapt and useless they had been. In the case of government employees, when they struck work, it was well nigh impossible for the police to function in their midst. A peon succumbed to injuries alleged to have been caused by the police. This was a signal for an agitation mounted by some political parties, to demonstrate against the high-handedness and callous behaviour of these minions of the law. These political leaders, mainly leftist, would not agree to the dead body being subjected to a postmortem even though the allegation was one of rough handling. This was a case of a consumptive collapsing suddenly after vomiting blood which was wrongly fastened to tackling by the police. I went along with the chief secretary and a minister to the cremation ground on the banks of Ganga and requested that the body be shown to the demonstrators. The procession was led by an eminent medical practitioner—a leader of the Communist party—but he would not agree to this for obvious reasons. The crowd attempted to mob me and stone my vehicle, apparently supporting the illogical stand of their leader. Such was the disenchantment with government that the people in general would accept any anti-establishment allegations. It was interesting that another political luminary also of the C.P.I., who had set the ball rolling in this matter, made himself scarce and would not show up though requested to. Perhaps he was afraid of being found out and had some qualms of conscience. He was a college pal of mine to boot.

Lack of respect for the policeman—there was no question of any fear, resulted in the entire police work becoming highly ineffective : otherwise the police was also functioning highly inefficiently. Police morale was also at a very low ebb and you could see this in any gathering and even at the street corner where policemen performed traffic control duty. They appeared to have no heart in their job, and allowed traffic rules to be violated and go unnoticed in their very presence. When questioned, the constable would say that this was the state of affairs in the country and he was entirely helpless.

The question of police ethics was discussed at a meeting of the Rotary Club which I was addressing in the capital. Earlier I had been elected unanimously to the august position of Governor of Rotary International, my area including Burma, Assam, West Bengal, Bihar, Orissa, eastern Madhya Pradesh, and Nepal and Bhutan; in fact the entire eastern part of India and Burma. I had to admit that there were political pressures on the police personnel at all levels, which would impinge on their efficiency. But this was the position in all democracies and fresh procedures had to be evolved so that the loyalty of the police was not subjective but to the law which they had to enforce. In this context the role of the armed police was important as the law and order situation in the country would not allow of the police force being made entirely a civil organisation. Japan had a separate riot police to keep order if demonstrations materialised. Yet, I was surprised that the press report about the meeting caused serious concern to some ministers who wanted that my explanation should be called for and a replacement should be found for this forthright officer. A special minus factor was that I had extra curricular interests like Rotary which was a service organisation par excellence far removed from any vestiges of politics ! No formal explanation was called for but I had to go into long sessions with the Chief Minister and the Deputy Chief Minister to discuss the issues involved, in particular the absence of appropriate public relations set-up in the police which made this force greatly misunderstood.

An atmosphere of intrigue seized the entire administration and the police were no exception. This had a special application to this department as police subordinates placed in the station houses were extremely useful to the high ups in Delhi and they were drawn into the vortex of the political game. Even the positioning of Assistant Sub-Inspectors of police saw wire pulling and interference from central ministers on peurile grounds. There was an undercurrent of feeling that if some positioning of subordinate police officers could be effected by the minister's interference, the local populace would be convinced of his importance. They would then possibly line up in their support and help in elections to the Panchayat, to local Municipal Committees, and even to party forums. The positioning of subordinate officers of the executive branch had assumed such important proportions that on the fall of one of the ministries headed by Bhola Paswan Shastri, he quite frankly told me in a private session—I had to see him daily in connection with my work—that his resignation was entirely due to the wrangle over the posting of a Block Development Officer.

Police work now depended greatly on support from local political bosses and this was available only on the basis of give and take. Another factor worth mentioning was that the common man could not understand the rationale of the police acting to keep up the authority of a local leader, when their job was law keeping. The elaborate arrangements made for the security of a VIP, who belonged to the area amused the people and even caused annoyance. The police therefore developed the image of a partisan group helping those already in power. This was not liked and violent demonstrations followed. Even peaceful working of the state legislatures was difficult. This fire was fanned by groups inside the government who were trying to edge into positions of vantage. As Churchill had stated on the eve of Indian independence, "men of chaff" were thrown up to positions of eminence, and it was galling for police officers to dance attendance on them.

The central Minister for Planning was scheduled to pay a visit to Dhanbad, where the Coal Mines Research Institute of India was located. Dhanbad is not on the air map and the local landing strip was then out of commission. The Minister and his party boarded the Rajdhani Express at Delhi, hoping to detrain at Dhanbad in due time, but a derailment on the grand chord sector, passing through Gaya and Dhanbad in Bihar, resulted in the train being diverted by what is known as the main-line via Patna. He realised at night that his train would be diverted via the State capital. Therefore the entire lot detrained at Patna. I was summoned early in the morning to the State Guest House where the Minister was sojourning. On reaching there I had to wait for the honourable minister as he was still in the bath-room. Later after a pow vow with him, I sent a message on the wireless to Dhanbad regarding the minister's journey by road. I was unhappy that for a petty item like this, which could be indicated on the phone to the state hospitality and protocol officer or even to my office—the office of the I.G. police, or the Chief Secretary's office, the minister considered it proper to summon me.

An ex-Chief Minister, though he was in this position for a few days only, was the main accused in a case of fraud connected with the starting of a medical college. An assurance was held out by the government on the floor of the Vidhan Sabha that the matter would be examined quickly and in particular the arrest of the ex-C.M. would be effected, if necessary. The Assurance Committee of the Legislature went into this matter while the case was still under investigation. The evidence took a little more time to be collected and gleaned to warrant arrest. Staying with a political big wig, now not a minister, the ex-C.M. was sought to be arrested by the investigating officer but he was warned to be prepared to face the consequence of his rash act. This threat included me also as the arrest could not have been made without my concurrence, when the matter was raised even before the Assurances Committee.

An incident which rocked the state and of which echoes were heard in the Lok Sabha also, was the attack on an Adivasi village by the minions of a local Rajput landlord in the district of Purnea. The D.I.G. police of this area was also a Rajput and the District S.P. was a Brahmin. The Rajput landlord was a much respected public leader who had earlier adorned the *gaddi* of the Speaker in the Vidhan Sabha. He was in a bad state of health but it was stated that under his directions, his *sipahis* had attacked the adivasis, burnt their hutments and killed quite a few of them. The Chief Minister then was himself a member of the Scheduled Caste, and known to be a close associate of the Rajput landlord. The case was pursued with due alacrity and the officers who were found remiss were suspended. Yet the court intrigue at Patna would over that high caste officers were soft pedalling the case. There was a visit by the Union Minister of State for Home Affairs Shri Ram Nivas Mirdha and efforts were made by the backward class lobby to din into his ears that the police under a Rajput (Khatri) I.G. had not acted promptly. The Chief Secretary belonged to the backward class, and perhaps gave the impression that the police may be acting in caste-grooves. The Adivasi element in the state Vidhan Sabha including Adivasi ministers sent for me and wanted action to be taken against the Rajput D.I.G. and the Brahmin S.P. It was my job to assuage their feeling and assure them that there was no question of the official machinery acting in a partisan manner. But such was the reputation of the establishment that I found it difficult to convince them of it. As for the Rajput landlord, he had to be placed under arrest in spite of his bad health as there appeared to be some material against him. There were stormy discussions in the Lok Sabha and I was happy that the position of my department was vindicated. I was told on good authority that the courtiers in the Raj Bhavan had decided that the police did act in a partisan manner under my leadership whatever may be made out by the available evidence. This was the impression that I carried after I had some discussions regarding the incident with the Rajyapal. There conclusions were that the Brahmin S.P. was acting under the influence of the Brahmin ex-Home Minister, while the Rajput complicity was under my guidance. I was told by friends that I may soon find an honoured place on the shelf and that a pliant incumbent for active control of police working was required.

Medals for meritorious and distinguished service have been awarded traditionally to the members of the police force, much in the style of the decorations given to members of the armed forces. The awards, the Indian Police Medal, and the King's Police Medal, were made after due consideration by a section of the Viceroy's secretariat. In regard to the King's Police Medal, these had to be approved in the Home Office. The usual channels of recommendation were adopted. With independence, all this work was done between the Home Ministry and the President's Secretariat at Delhi. The recommendations coming from the effective police wings which included states and the central police forces had merely to be reviewed centrally. As these awards carried some financial benefit for the subordinate staff, considerable jockeying for positions was in evidence. Now officers, whose names were not recommended by the primary echelons, started obtaining these distinctions by having their names inserted in the lists at higher levels. A public statement was made by the Home Minister in Bihar that lower ranks in the force should receive weightage in these awards as in the case of the scheduled castes and tribes getting weightages in appointments according to the country's Constitution. There was thus a complete disarray in the awards of these medals. However, on receipt of the recommendations, I sent up the names of those who were deserving of the awards. I was surprised to have a visit from Swami Harinarayan and, an important leader of the Bharat Sewak Samaj and Bharat Sadhu Samaj. He unabashedly pointed out that he had learnt of my recommendations for police medals and that he was disappointed to find that no recommendations had been made for any Bhumihar officer. He thought that I had put in names of some Rajput officers. The implication according to him was that : a Rajput (Khatri) from Punjab had pushed up Rajput cases in preference to the better deserving Bhumihars. He even named some senior Bhumihar police officers who deserved to get these medals. I had made no such evaluation by caste of the persons to be recommended. I asked Swamiji how he came to get the information and could he vouch for its authenticity. He had apparently got the information through some of his sources in the secretariat, particularly the Bhumihar police officers in the police headquarters. Swami Harinarayananand was a Bhumihar but having donned the saffron attire, he was expected to have no caste affiliations. This demonstration of caste-bias from a personage of the holy order caused me not a little surprise. The Swami was the subject of considerable controversy when he was appointed as Chief of the State anti Corruption Board a little later. He had been holding seminars on the subject regularly inviting central dignitaries and was a forceful speaker on the ills of casteism and the corruption that this could generate. Yet the Swami even stated that it bode ill for my tenure as the police chief of the state, by making the recommendations that I had made ! Irked by this, I made enquiries and found that in collusion with the secretariat brass, the names of other officers including some Bhumihar officers, were included in the state list sent to the central government. This feat in the secretariat, which was a complete derogation of the code of discipline to which the police should be wedded, incensed me greatly and I made a point of it to the Chief Minister. The Chief Minister had apparently had no time to read through the file and had approved of the names forwarded by the Chief Secretary ! He was bland enough to agree that he would check up on future lists sent by me. However, the Chief Minister was soon to demit office and his honest intentions could not be translated into practice. On my part, I made a visit to Delhi and impressed on the authorities processing the case, to cut out the names not recommended by me. They were not aware of the names that I had sent up. Having known the details, these new names inserted by the secretariat were removed from the list which had to go to the President's Secretariat for approval. The officers whose names had been put in, as also the secretariat brass in Patna had the shock of their lives when the award of medals was declared by Delhi. I am sure the most disappointed person was Swami Harinarayananand who should have realised that this tampering with departmental procedure was not so easy if the police chief was vigilant. Obviously he had made the mistake of disclosing to me the views of the caste coterie in the state and the possibility of tampering with my recommendations.

A system which was in vogue during the earlier dispensation was of having what was grandiloquently called the *darbar*. This was held at divisional level and awards were given here. In the police the S.P. held a darbar in which police subordinates could air their personal or group grievances. This institution was continued even after independence. But now ministers started holding their own darbars and this became a daily feature. The routine was to have a large concourse of people meet in a hall in the large ministerial residences. Some officials were also called up. To obtain access to this darbar, it was incumbent to obtain the approval or connivance of the personal staff of the minister, who could arrange for seats of vantage so as to catch the eye of the big one when he marched in. The din and pandemonium which was generated was symbolic of the democracy that had been ushered in the country! Police matters were discussed threadbare in such darbars and this denigrated the police in the eyes of the common people. It was a sight to see senior officers behaving like liveried attendants though they strutted about the countryside as bosses. Detailed discussion of important files could be held here and sometimes the minister would troop out with a favourite officer to give him a private audience, which was more to make a recommendation to him. All this showed to the minister's clientele, that "powerful" officials were under his thumb and would kowtow to his personal preferences.

Towards the end of 1971, conditions had become so confusing in Bihar that President's rule had to be imposed once again. This spell of President's rule, with a powerful centre, had a different complexion. Raj Bhavan became the centre of all activity. The Rajyapal, now functioned without the help of any adviser. He started off by making large scale changes of the administrative heads. This was done to impress on stipendiary officers that they had to toe the "central" line. Even the state liaison officer in Delhi, a Commissoner, was changed overnight for no special reason. A special Committee for revising police regulations was set up, a matter which should have awaited the result of the elections to be held shortly. Even though the custodian of the interests of the permanent services, he was reported to be touring about and threatening the subordinate officers including S.Ps that they would be transferred to inhospitable posts if they failed to show up according to his expectations. I was informed that some S.Ps were told by the Rajyapal that the state I.G. should also mind his step as it was a simple matter transferring him to an innocuous job, which could be created. The rude shock caused in police circles, was obvious. L.N. Mishra, Lalit Babu to most of his friends, was then a Minister of State in the Central Cabinet and was looking after the portfolio of Commerce and Foreign Trade. He staked his claim to the seat in the Lok Sabha rendered vacant by the passing away of Pt. Binodanand Jha, an erstwhile Chief Minister of Bihar who had been inducted in the central sphere in the elections in 1971. Lalit Babu was so far a member of the Rajya Sabha and this election would have meant for him an upward march in the government at Delhi. The lavish election campaign launched by him would be long remembered in Bihar. The police arrangements were far too elaborate and yet Lalit Babu showed his preference for the induction of the army also. He made requests for various changes in the positioning of police officers down to the level of A.S.I., right on the eve of the contest. This was not possible for me to accede to and its result was that I was translated to the job of Chairman of the State Police Reorganisation Committee only two days before the date of the elections. Such changes were not permissible according to the Election Commissions directions and to add, the state was then under President's rule when observance of central directions should have been more meticulous.

I was happy at having been rid of the job of the state I.G. Police and hoped that now some constructive work could perhaps be possible in my new assignment. However, I was not able to relish the suddenness with which the change was made in violation of the accepted norms. The constabulary threatened to go on strike but I most emphatically indicated to the Policemen's Union not to do any such thing. It would have been definitely construed as my handiwork. And I was most anxious not to get involved in any controversy. I felt that it was my duty to serve in whatever appropriate capacity the government intended to utilise my talents ; but it should not mean any derogation to the rank held by me. These happenings did little credit to the system and the matter was persistently raised in the new Vidhan Sabha of the state for which the elections took place a few months later. This also resulted in a precipitate down grade in the morale of the police particularly at the higher levels : no officer felt safe in regard to his position and prospects.

In my new job, I was to get extra allowances also and I could do some work which would leave its "footprints on the sands of time". An officials' committee was also appointed to assist me but these officials did not have the time to give to this work.

Interestingly an I.P.S. officer, who had resigned and had joined politics while yet young in service and who had served under me in various capacities, was also named as a member. After the duties in the state I had the committee expanded by including new members. It included an erstwhile Deputy Speaker (an ex-Vice Chancellor) of the assembly and Mr. Fazlur Rehman later to be a minister at the centre in the Janata government formed at Delhi in 1977. I also discussed the matter with the government to find out how far they were prepared to go. Yet I found the government extremely lukewarm to anything being done. It was a difficult task even organising an office for this committee. Finding that the progress was slow I made pilgrimage to the central founts of authority to brief myself in detail about the circumstances leading to my elevation to the special post. The Home Secretary had made a visit to the state on the eve of the bye-election, palpably to study the arrangements made. He had not discussed the issues with me. Therefore as relinquishing charge, I met the Home Secretary, who also disclaimed any hand in the transfers and yet wanted to know the trend of the affair in regard to the opposition leaders. I pieced up the happenings in Bihar with the goings on in Delhi where the Director of the Intelligence Bureau had been elevated to the job of Vice Chairman of the Police Recruitment and Training Committee. The position was the same all over the country.

In the new style of functioning the Inspector General of Police had virtually to act as an A.D.C. of the politician who came to occupy the *gaddi* of the Home Minister or Chief Minister. This was so for some time but the position was definitely worse. The District Superintendent of Police had to behave in the same way with the local luminaries including the district representative in the state cabinet. In the brief President's rule before 1972 state elections, the state Rajyapal did not appear to act any differently. Most unseemly incidents had occured during this peroid. A Deputy Inspector General of police, was suspended and departmental proceedings were due to be started against him on the curiously grave charge of continuing to stay in government accommodation though required to vacate it. This was disputed by the D.I.G, but being a meek type he shifted to tents pitched in front of his house on the roadside land. He later suffered a heart attack and succumbed to it, obviously the resultant of the peculiar treatment meted out to him. Another D.I.G., who later rose to be the Director General of

C.R.P.F., was likewise proposed to be suspended and proceeded against. This was done at the instance of the new police leadership out to harass those who they considered were not "committed". This officer suffered, this indignity of suspension for a few days only. I witnessed these developments from my new position of vantage. About twenty five years after independence, the police department was in complete shambles and in fact the general comment was that this was not a force but a farce.

As noted earlier, 1972 elections brought in a new Congress government in the state but the administration was on a track far removed from what it should have been. The party leader was selected by the Congress High Command by what was called consensus, which meant that the group in the Vidhan Sadha was led up the garden path by the central leadership. All and sundry made the pilgrimage to Delhi. On various occasions the state cabinet meetings could be convened at Delhi. There were even occasions when almost all the M.L.As were at Delhi. To find a berth in the airlines or on the train to Delhi from Patna was a difficult task. Nehru had likened the Bihar political crowd as "Bhatiaras". Then this statement was much disliked. But now its appropriateness was more than apparent. The security of life and property was at a low level in the state. The atmosphere of duplicity made even the shadow suspect. The public disapprobation of the goings on was spearheaded by the students and youth aiming at unsettling the government with a view to having fresh polls. In this process state ministers, known to be corrupt, and inefficient, were surrounded and adorned with bangles and vermillion suited for the womenfolk. The young men expected that the ministers would tender resignation as an aftermath of these incidents but that was not to be. The thesis was to stick to the seats of authority whatever the public feeling. In these demonstrations the police proved highly ineffective and earned a bad name both from the ruling political leaders and the opposing group. The demonstrators even *gheraoed* the Assembly building and the Secretariat making normal work impossible. Not able to assess the situation and actuated by narrow considerations, the government could only make changes in the top police echelons. The Inspectors General were changed in quick succession. One Inspector General was changed within a period of three months. During his stewardship a demonstration in front of the Vidhan Sabha turned violent and police had to fire on them. The Inspector General came to the demonstrating crowd and followed the usual drill of firing tear smoke squibs followed by resort to live-fire. The Chief Minister, however, did not want this to be done resulting in the situation going out of hand and the firing being resorted to with delay. Obviously the I.G. was not at fault but the treatment meted out to him led to a complete demoralisation of the police force. The situation was like a battle being fought with various leaders each trying to fasten the blame for the inevitable debacle on the other. However, another incident in which Jaya Prakash Narayan was beaten up during a protest demonstration, was slurred over quite intentionally.

The anti-government demonstrations had a direct impact on me. I was proceeding to my office in a staff car on one of these days but had to return because of a complete siege there. The rowdies hurled missiles on the car and the police driver was badly hurt but managed to extricate the car. I noticed that the malcontents bore victory marks on their forehead like the Rajput warriors of old going out for battle. These reinforcements to the demonstration were obtained from Rajasthan area, but I was amused to find that all enquiries completely omitted this and got embroiled in local conflicts. The house of a D.I.G. was also ransacked and looted by the demonstrators but nothing could be done to stave it off. The more important aspect was that this was within hail and view of police guards in the secretariat building. The demonstrations were unsurpassed in their vehemence so far but it was fantastic that the establishment should ignore it and remain practically inactive.

In all this confusion a mighty *yagna* was arranged near Giridih, centre of the mica mining and allied industries. The moving spirit behind it was Chandraswami of Andhra, a tantric who prided himself on being a close confidant of one of the PM's aides. Huge sums of money were collected and a tented township grew up on the site of the *yagna* The state government planes at Patna were now performing taxi service to and from Giridih of which the *kutcha* runway got a face-lift. Funds for this purpose made available though other developmental works were practically at a standstill. The political top brass of the Congress in the state vied with each other to get closer to the Swami who was considered to be one of the minor circle at the centre. The publication in the weekly *Blitz* did a lot to prick the balloon but this was somewhat of a cry in the wilderness. I was dismayed at the way top police formations got embroiled in this game. They even looked for other tantrics so that the tune may be continued even though one Swami would leave the scene. Top police officers accompanied the Minister of State for Police for no palpable reasons. Naturally questions were asked in the Vidhan Sabha regarding the part played by police officers in settling the household affairs of the concerned ministers in order to gain their support and confidence. A more important aspect of the new elections which had brought the Congress back to power in the state, though with a greatly decimated strength, was the complexion of the money-bags who acted in their support. Election had become an expansive and even more expensive exercise with the march ahead of democracy in the country. With the economy staying poor, the raising of the funds for fighting out elections has presented problems, which though not entirely new has facets of interest. Ganja smuggling has been an old game in north Bihar, carrying the weed from Nepal Tarai to markets in Calcutta and Bombay and even to other countries. In this game Kamdeo Singh of the Begusarai sub-division of the District of Monghyr, had become a legendary figure. He was known to be baiting politicians and thereby warding off the processes of law. He was known to have actively participated in gruesome murders and his hide-out in Begusarai was difficult of access. His informants gave him all the news to enable him to keep away from public functionaries that could not be inveigled by him in his tentacles. I had initiated a plan for capturing him and was informed that he had escaped into Nepal—some stories even said that he had perished due to wounds received in an encounter with the police. There was an encounter on the river Ganga as well, in which he had perhaps been drowned. But in the latest elections, Kamdeo was reported acting in concert with some of the Congress party candidates and this was brought up in the Vidhan Sabha, which met after the elections. This information was no plus-point for the newly elected Congress legislators, specially some of the ministers who were specifically arraigned of hobnobbing with the arch Ganja smuggler.

There was a further recrudescence of communal trouble about this time, a phenomenon which had cropped up earlier but now there was an added vehemence. While in 1947, the Muslim minority appeared to be disorganised and demoralised for various reasons, the recent elections had demonstrated the importance of unity of purpose basing on religion rather than political ideology or economic constraints. The jingoists even talked of the Muslim community in India asking for a new parcel as their homeland, on the lines of Pakistan which was already achieved. Some analysts attributed the communal incidents, and some of them in Madhya Pradesh and Bihar were indeed gruesome, to the offensive behaviour of the minority community like the rape of a Hindu girl by Muslim goondas or interference with routines of Hindu worship or even marriages. The commissions of enquiry, which were set up, made various suggestions, but the government did not have the heart in the work in view of the developing opposition. The ground was slipping from under feet. The more unsatisfactory aspect of the new situation was that any incident howsoever minor, was foisted on the local subordinate staff. The standard question asked would be, what were the police deployments earlier and what deployments were made on the occasion in reference. Any reduction in police strength would evoke the question that inadequate protection was afforded. Police methodology in dealing with communal riots or other incidents was now merely a matter of overemphasising what was already in vogue. But the earlier arrangements had been thoroughly discredited ! The entire responsibility of the senior formations was also sought to be transferred to a large body of armed subordinates who had no special training or even the capacity to act if any serious discussion took place. Police placing therefore became a mockery, and additionally the burden on the public exchequer became heavier.

In the field of crimes, the conventional crimes went completely out of hand. Attempts were made from time to time to make comparative statistical studies by making comparisons with other states and countries to show averages and to indicate that the position everywhere was quite satisfactory ! Very often the rise in population was used as an argument to show that there was no increase worth the name. The fact, however, remained that the number of crimes particularly those involving use of violence went up by leaps and bounds. Particularly serious cases of the barbaric type like dacoities and robberies showed colossal increases: this notwithstanding the device adopted of not recording cases or even burking them. The result of the investigation was just as unsatisfactory and it was stated that the hands of the investigators were full with other law and order duties. The police had in fact become a thoroughly discredited law keeping force with no time for investigation of conventional crimes. The number of cases pending investigation mounted so much that it was a job even to collect statistics of such cases.

About this time the entire government in the State of Bihar was in a state of paralysis, thanks to the popular movement which had been started. These movements correctly aimed at the jingoism of the centre and its interference in the state's affairs. It was incontrovertible that government in the states led by the Congress party, was much worse than what prevailed for example in the state of Tamilnadu, now under the D.M.K. The police had now become the hand-maiden of the politician. This service was required to perform all odd jobs including keeping vigil at private entertainment functions, and accompanying the political leaders. The turn-out of the man in uniform already bad, went worse and became an object of derision. The police was compared now to the pioneer corps, whose job was to do sweeping and furbishing chores.

I had nothing to do actively with the goings on and the poor standards of performance and behaviour of the police. Attempting to make a thorough job of the reorganisation and the preparation of a new police regulations manual for the state police, I pressed forward with the work and took the state M.Ps in confidence but I was told to go on much as 1 liked as the possibility of any major recommendation being processed and adopted was bleak. Undeterred, I went ahead with the refrain of Gurudev Rabindra Nath Tagore in which he had exhorted that one should do it alone, if others failed. I presented to the chief minister of the state—by now Abdul Ghafoor had come to occupy this position—three big volumes of regulations and details of reorganisation of the police in the state. The C.M. wanted that I should have an extension in service to be able to implement the recommendations made by me. This was palpably absurd as I could not function as the ultimate judge of my own work. The report therefore continues to remain on the anvil of the secretariat.

On the eve of my retirement from the Indian Police, the senior officers at the state headquarters got together a dinner party to bid farewell. I had spurned offers of lucrative employment in the private sector and had not accepted any extension in government employ as well. The reason was the sad state of discipline in the country with a complete crisis of confidence. I referred to this in my valedictory address and pointed to the black sheep in the police, who had created conditions of near chaos in the department. Unfortunately their number in the superior cadres was much larger than in the lowest rung that is the constabulary. The loyalty and sense of duty of the constabulary was the strong point of the police when I started in it. This was still not so bad but the superior cadres gave me the jitters because of their inept behaviour. I had started in the I.P. thirty six years ago when it was an effective and well-disciplined force. With all its faults, the oppressive methods adopted, and the corruption, it was a useful vehicle of public service and fulfilled its task. But now the scene was that of a misshapen mass, larger numerically, particularly in sectors where they were little required, highly ineffective, and divorced from the people whom they were to serve. This is the police service of the democratic republic of India, which has been evolved through three decades of independence.

I recorded some of these points in a book captioned the *Indian Police*, which was in fact a case of loud thinking on police problems. It was published in 1978, three years after my retirement. A National Police Commission had also been set up by the post emergency Janata government in 1977. How far this can help ameliorate the sorry state of affairs, is a moot question. After all police is a subject on the state list and the recommendations of this Commission will require processing by each state government, already armed with reports of their own Police Commissions, which have remained in cold storage. To my mind the conclusions are writ large on the walls that we would continue to blunder. The mutiny in the police forces which has supervened has not acted to rouse us from somnolence. I do hope that we avoid falling into chaos. Did not Lord Krishna say in the Gita that when the rule of law is likely to become defunct, He would incarnate Himself to save the country and the Indian society? Let us hope and pray for the best.

INDEX